Aspec

SOCIA

GENER

John Barron Mays
Eleanor Rathbone Professor of Sociology
University of Liverpool

Maurice Craft
Professor of Education
University of Nottingham

Data collection in context

STEPHEN ACKROYD B.A., M.Sc.
Lecturer in Sociology
University of Lancaster

and

JOHN A. HUGHES B.Soc.Sc., Ph. D.
Senior Lecturer in Sociology
University of Lancaster

Longman London and New York

General Editors

John Barron Mays Professor of Sociology, University of Liverpool
Maurice Craft Professor of Education, University of Nottingham

This Longman library of texts in modern sociology consists of three Series, and includes the following titles:

THE SOCIAL STRUCTURE OF MODERN BRITAIN

The family
Mary Farmer
University of Liverpool

The political structure
Grace Jones
King Alfred's College,
Winchester

Population
Prof. R. K. Kelsall
University of Sheffield

Education
Ronald King
University of Exeter

The welfare state
Prof. David Marsh
University of Nottingham

Crime and its treatment
Prof. John Barron Mays
University of Liverpool

Patterns of urban life
Prof. R. E. Pahl
University of Kent

The working class
Kenneth Roberts
University of Liverpool

The middle class
John Raynor
The Open University

Leisure
Kenneth Roberts
University of Liverpool

Adolescence
Cyril Smith
Social Science Research Council

The mass media
Peter Golding
University of Leicester

The legal structure
Michael Freeman
University of London

Rural life
Gwyn Jones
University of Reading

Religious institutions
Joan Brothers
University of London

Mental illness
Bernard Ineichen
University of Bristol

Forthcoming titles will include:

Minority groups
Eric Butterworth
University of York

The economic structure
Prof. Cedric Sandford
University of Bath

SOCIAL PROCESSES

Bureaucracy
Dennis Warwick
University of Leeds

Social control
C. Ken Watkins
University of Leeds

Communication
Prof. Denis McQuail
University of Amsterdam

Stratification
Prof. R. K. Kelsall
University of Sheffield
and
H. Kelsall

Industrialism
Barry Turner
University of Exeter

Social change
Anthony Smith
University of Reading

Socialisation
Graham White
University of Liverpool

Social Conflict
Prof. John Rex
University of Warwick

Forthcoming titles will include:

Migration
Prof. J. A. Jackson
University of Dublin

SOCIAL RESEARCH

The limitations of social research
Prof. M. D. Shipman
University of Warwick

Social research design
Prof. E. Krausz
University of Newcastle
and
S. H. Miller
City University

Sources of official data
Kathleen Pickett
University of Liverpool

History of social research methods
Gary Easthope
University of East Anglia

Deciphering data
Jonathan Silvey
University of Nottingham

The philosophy of social research
John Hughes
University of Lancaster

Data collection in context
Stephen Ackroyd
and
John Hughes
University of Lancaster

Longman Group Limited,
Longman House,
Burnt Mill, Harlow, Essex, UK

*Published in the United States of America
by Longman Inc., New York*

First published 1981

British Library Cataloguing in Publication Data

Ackroyd, Stephen
    Data collection in context. – (Aspects of
modern sociology: social research).
    1. Social sciences – Methodology
    I. Title   II. Hughes, John A
    300'.72   H61   80–41701

    ISBN 0-582-48015-9

Printed in Singapore by Four Strong Printing Co

CONTENTS

EDITORS' PREFACE

The first series in Longman's *Aspects of Modern Sociology* library was concerned with the social structure of modern Britain, and was intended for students following professional and other courses in universities, polytechnics, colleges of education, and elsewhere in further and higher education, as well as for those members of a wider public wishing to pursue an interest in the nature and structure of British society.

This further series sets out to examine the history, aims, techniques and limitations of social research, and it is hoped that it will be of interest to the same readership. It will seek to offer an informative but not uncritical introduction to some of the methodologies of social science.

John Barron Mays
Maurice Craft

FOREWORD

In this book we have tried to avoid competing with the many, some of them excellent, texts which discuss at great length all the finer detail of social research methods. The reasons for this are not entirely due to limitations of space. Instead, we have tried to approach methods of data collection from a slightly different angle by looking at what we term, the 'social context of method'. Accordingly, although the reader will find a brief account of the orthodox prescriptions of the main data collection methods, we have tried to move the discussion further by looking at these as social theories masquerading, too often, as a technology of data. We have also attempted to cast a little light on the wider social and cultural factors which affect the intellectual authority of a particular method.

We have substantially limited ourselves to a discussion of two of the major methods of data collection, namely, the social survey and interview, and participant observation. The reason for this is mainly to effect a starker comparison. But it should not be forgotten that many of the questions and issues we raise are pertinent to other methods.

Finally, we should like to thank a number of people who have helped in the preparation of this book. First the editors and the publisher for their patience. Second, Brenda, Pam and Jacky for urgent typing services when sorely needed. Third, Pam and Jacky, again, for not minding too much about our neglect of parental duties. Mark Stevens is owed a debt for keeping an important research project going while the final drafts of the book were completed. We should also like to thank our other colleagues, friends and students for providing an interesting and challenging social and intellectual milieu in which to work. If they have not been as supportive and understanding at times as we would have liked, charity suggests that this is due to what they perceive as the tedium of our chosen subject. We hope that this book will go some way towards relieving the dreadful boredom which descends when research methods come up for discussion. As we suggest here methods of data collection deserve, even demand, the serious attention of social scientists as a subject of study to which the theories and insights of social science apply.

Stephen Ackroyd
John A. Hughes

BY THE SAME AUTHOR

John A. Hughes

Political Sociology (*1972*)
Sociological Analysis: methods of discovery (*1976*)
The Philosophy of Social Research (*1980*)

1

DATA AND RESEARCH PRACTICE

Methods are ways of getting things done which is one reason, perhaps, why many social scientists tend to view social research methods as merely practical activities of no great importance in the intellectual scheme of things, and certainly secondary to the more abstract kinds of theoretical work. For much the same kind of reason methods are often not regarded as a suitable specialism for a serious social scientist but rather an activity that is best left to experts in the technology involved. A concern for methods of data collection and analysis is frequently delegated to tame statisticians or computer programmers who generously give their time and skills to advise social scientists on appropriate methods of data collection and analysis. To this extent, social scientists have fallen victim to the recent tremendous growth in the technology of data processing which, rightly or wrongly, they feel has moved into arcane realms far beyond their own special competence.

Certainly the technology for creating and handling information has reached an unprecedented level in the history of human society. The symbol of this information explosion is the computer: a machine capable of processing truly prodigious amounts of information in the blink of an eye. Businessmen, market researchers, social workers, police forces, academic researchers, governments, and more, are all eager, for various reasons, to use this capacity of the computer to process large amounts of information exceedingly quickly. Yet, while the technology itself and the operations it can perform are indeed complicated beyond the imagining of ordinary mortals, neither of these facts constitutes a good reason for regarding research methods as technical matters beyond our concern. For one thing, it is important to recognise that a computer, unlike the research methods it sometimes serves, is only a machine tool. It is a tool usable in social research only in so far as what it is capable of doing is relevant to the research goals. Simply because such a wonderful technology is available is no reason for presuming that all social research requires the assistance of a computer. One of the irritations of our age is the justification often offered by TV reporters that the results of some study showing that vandalism has increased tenfold in X town were analysed by computer, as if this alone validated or guaranteed the scientific status of the study concerned. Moreover, even if a computer is useful for some research, the results it produces can only be as good as the initial data it is given and the programs it is asked to perform on that data. In other words, before machine processing becomes even a possibility the phenomena of the world, to put it this way, have to be turned into appropriate data.

Our subject concerns the methods and techniques of data collection as used in the social sciences, especially sociology. To this extent we are concerned with the techniques used by social scientists to generate data. However else one may regard the social sciences they are both theoretical and empirical activities. They aim to explain, by means of theory, the phenomena of the social world.[1] The link between theory and the empirical world is provided, in large part, by research; that is, by examining the empirical world in a systematic way in order to assess the accuracy, truth, adequacy, plausibility, etc. of theories. If we exclude purely theoretical research, which can be as important as the empirical variety, research results in data. From our point of view, data are very much the outcome, the creation even, of empirical research. Data, of whatever form, do not just appear or lie around waiting to be casually picked up by some passing researcher. In a strong sense of the word, data has to be created. Our concern in this book will be that part of this process of data creation to do with the collection rather than the analysis of data; though, clearly, the two stages are not unconnected. Indeed, as we shall see in connection with participant observation methods, data collection and analysis of necessity have to proceed in conjunction with one another in order to make the method work at all. This is not quite true of the other methods we shall be discussing, such as the survey, where the stage of data analysis has to await the collection and coding of a considerable number of questionnaires. In this particular case data analysis has indeed become an expertise in its own right. However, for our purposes, though the distinction between data collection and data analysis is somewhat artificial, our emphasis will be on methods of collection rather than analysis.

The process of creating data entails treating what we might call the things of the everyday world rather differently from ways in which they are likely to be treated by the ordinary everyday observer. Natural science has shown us how complex even ordinary physical objects are. One has only to think about how a chemist might describe the molecular structure of the paper on which this book is printed to appreciate this point. Moreover, such a chemical description would not exhaust all that it is possible to say about the paper. Indeed, a number of descriptions could be made of the paper depending upon the point of view or the purpose of the observer. Nor need these descriptions necessarily be alternatives but could complement each other. A printer's concern, say, with the quality of the paper might well lead on to consideration of its chemistry, the raw materials used to produce it, and perhaps even its physics. The point is that each of our onlookers would notice rather different things about the paper and, accordingly, identify or emphasise different qualities for further detailed examination. Data are always the result of a selection from what can possibly be said about some phenomenon. This is as true of the phenomena of the natural sciences as it is of the social sciences. With regard to the latter, the living, breathing, happy, sad people we know in our daily lives are not, in this form, data; they are merely the source of data. To become data, or to be reconstituted as data, they need to be placed within some theoretical framework that informs research.

Theory and methods of research

The orthodox image of research in social science is taken very much from what is perceived as the practice of natural science.

Research is carried out to test hypotheses which, in turn, are derived from various theories offered to explain some feature of the physical world. One of the major criteria of a good theory is its ability to predict events in the empirical world. If it fails to do this, whatever other qualities it might possess are simply otiose. There are, of course, other conceptions of the research process, a common one being that research is carried out to discover new 'facts'. Here the model might be the archaeologist digging deeper into some mound of earth to discover something new about a little-known civilisation, or an astronomer building a better telescope to see further into the far reaches of the universe. Both of these models of the research process, as far as they go, seem adequate enough. However, matters are not quite so simple and to see how they are more complicated let us make some preliminary points.

Whatever model of empirical research we adopt, what is clear is that we need instruments and techniques to gather the data or information deemed necessary to meet the aims of the research, whatever these may be. Thus, the physicist has at his, or her, disposal a vast armoury of instrumentation to record data, from the simple ruler and thermometer to the incomprehensibles of the electron microscope and the particle accelerator. Similarly, the social scientist has at his, or her, disposal such techniques or instruments of research as questionnaires, attitude scales, tape- and video-recorders, methods of participant observation, official statistics, and so forth. So, fairly obviously, research requires instruments for the recording of data. But, notice that in the by no means exhaustive examples given above the physicist and the social scientist do not usually use the same instruments. A physicist might, we suppose, use a tape- or video-recorder, but would not use them for the same purpose as a social scientist. The reasons for this are not hard to find. For one thing the disciplines deal with different phenomena and, hence, need to develop instruments of research particularly suited to their respective subject-matters. This issue, of course, has been a recurrent one in social thought for many hundreds of years and different implications for the study of human social life have been drawn from it. The issue itself depends upon a distinction made between the human world and the non-human world; the latter being the special province of natural science, the former of the human sciences. The distinction is held to be an important one as far as knowledge is concerned because of the unique properties possessed by human beings. Above all else they have language which makes possible the development of cultures and societies. Some social thinkers claimed that this distinction puts humanity beyond the scope of scientific inquiry, at least beyond the model presupposed by the natural sciences. Human action, that is, cannot be studied in the same way that one studies inanimate nature.[2] The knowledge we require, indeed can have, of human social life is of a different order to that knowledge produced by natural science. Others, however, have not taken this dichotomy so radically, arguing, instead, that though the human and the physical world are very different they can, none the less, be studied using the same logic of inquiry.

But whatever one's stand on this particular issue the point is that research instruments or techniques used for collecting and creating data are sensitive to the nature of the phenomena that are the subject-matter of the discipline. This relationship between an instrument and the empirical world it is used to investigate is established through what we might call, 'instrumental presuppositions'. At its simplest, this notion refers to the conceptions a scientific community holds about what enables a particular instrument or technique to do the job for which it is used; in other words, theories about the kind of data an instrument, whatever it might be, generates. In physics, for example, temperatures can be measured by an ordinary mercury thermometer or by electronic means. Distance can be measured by an ordinary tape measure or by the time it takes light to travel from one point to another. In each case the instrument is seen to work because it embodies various kinds of theories in its construction as an instrument.[3] The same is also true of the research instruments used in social research. As we shall see in subsequent chapters, questionnaires, for example, derive their status as research instruments from conceptions held by their users of the relationship between the spoken word and social behaviour. Both natural and social scientists are committed to various sorts of instrumental presuppositions that underpin their research methods and techniques. These describe how a particular research instrument does its job. We shall, of course, discuss many of these instrumental presuppositions in the course of this book.

Closely related to these instrumental presuppositions – indeed they differ mainly in their scope and generality – are the explicit theories belonging to a particular discipline. These, too, contain implications for research methodology, though of a grosser kind than the instrumental theories discussed earlier. It is no accident that styles of sociological research are closely associated with particular theoretical perspectives. The survey, for example, grew out of a tradition which, among other things, claimed that the proper application of the scientific method to the study of society could result in the rational reconstruction of society for the benefit of all.[4] The major advantages of the survey, its ability to reach many thousands of people widely distributed in space, the statistical analyses that can be performed on its data, the use of various kinds of experimental designs in its conception, and so on, places it very clearly in the tradition which sees social science as following the path already trodden so firmly by the natural sciences. But, more specifically than this, the survey method also takes extremely seriously the idea of a social collectivity that can be studied by means of selected informants, so that the analyst can move between the behaviour of the individuals composing the collectivity to those larger social forces which cause individuals to behave more uniformly as parts of larger groups. This kind of sociological theory was most clearly put forward by Durkheim in his study of suicide, though he did not make use of the social survey method, where he endeavoured to show that suicide, at first glance the most asocial of behaviours, was related to social factors reaching beyond the individual and which could only be properties of the collectivity, or society.[5] Of course, once a conception such as this became firmly entrenched within social theory, the previous justifications of social surveys had to be rethought, as we shall see in Chapter 3.

So any sociological theory whether we are speaking of conflict theory, functionalism, Marxism, or whatever, will, inevitably, point an investigator to data relevant to the subject-matter of the theory. This is so not simply in the sense that if one is test-

ing some aspect of conflict theory one will need to investigate
conflicts, but also in the sense that the concepts in the theory
will make some specifications about what in the empirical world
are to count as conflicts. Are we to be concerned, say, only with
political conflicts or do we include things such as strikes,
divorces, elections and so on? But more than matters such as
these are involved, important as they are. All sociological
theories imply a conception of the individual, society, and the
relationship between the two. They could not do otherwise.
These conceptions also have implications for the method of
studying social life. If, for example, one is committed to a
sociological theory, such as symbolic interactionism, which sees
social interaction as a formative process in which the members of
society are continually engaged in 'directing, checking, bend-
ing, and transforming their lines of action in the light of what
they encounter in the actions of others', then one's research
instruments and activities will need to take this conception very
seriously.[6] Methods of research will be needed to capture this
image of the actor, which, because of its nature, the survey is
unlikely to be able to achieve satisfactorily.

Social theory, of course, is not the central concern of this
book which intends to deal with methods of data collection in
social science and particularly sociology. But it is of primary
importance to the subject of this book. Methods, or sometimes
methodology, are normally taken as covering what have been
referred to here as the technical aspects of research and dealing
with questions about how one constructs a questionnaire
schedule, or an attitude scale, conducts an interview, or draws a
random sample. To this extent methods and the techniques of
data collection designate the business end of a much more complicated piece of machinery. The remainder of the machine, and
essential to its working, are the 'instrumental' and 'theoretical'
presuppositions we have just been discussing. No method or
technique is atheoretical, but involves the user in a host of
theoretical commitments, many of them implicit, which reach
up to the most fundamental assumptions of the discipline.[7]
Many of these fundamental presuppositions are, in the social
sciences, moral in nature. It is this omnirelevance of values
which is often taken as another distinguishing feature of social

scientific research. Social scientists often research into matters that are also the deeply felt concerns of lay members of society. One has only to think of researches into social class, education, industrial behaviour, poverty, to mention but a few, to realise this. The social scientist, too, is a member of a society and, accordingly, could be said to share these concerns which, in turn, could well affect his or her research efforts. It might be that research has policy implications which may or may not be palatable to significant sections of society. In both these ways, and more, values are of ever present relevance for social scientific research and another route through which research methods reach up to our most fundamental conceptions of humankind.[8]

We have referred to the theoretical ideas which underpin and impinge on research techniques as presuppositions mainly because they are rarely formulated explicitly as theories. This tendency is associated with the trend in recent years for a minority of social scientists to concentrate their energies on becoming experts in methods which, in its turn, has led to the often impressive refinement of methods of data analysis, research, design, and in all branches of statistical testing. Such is the degree of this development that, as we suggested earlier, it has become difficult for any one person to master thoroughly all the available techniques, let alone have some expertise in other more substantive branches of the relevant discipline. A reason, again, for many to leave methods to statisticians and/or computer programmers. However, it should not be forgotten that methods, as the generic name should imply but often fails to do so in practice, are a means to an end, namely, better grounded social scientific knowledge. Quite what 'better grounded social scientific knowledge' should look like is an issue beyond method but still of vital importance. This can be seen in the patterns of change which typify the use of methods in social research. It is typically the case that theoretical developments in the discipline produce arguments justifying the considerable advantages to be gained from the employment of a particular method of research. Efforts are expended by the persuaded to refine and develop the method further until, some time later, it becomes widely felt that the returns from the method are diminishing and that some new kind of data would pay richer dividends. At this point the presuppositions of a method are subjected to stricter scrutiny, inconsistencies identified, the instrumental theories themselves may be discredited, and so forth. And it is not uncommon for major theoretical developments to result from such scrutinies. A recent case of this is the way in which ethnomethodology arose partly out of growing dissatisfactions expressed about the instrumental presuppositions of such methods as the interview. This questioning opened up the very basic issue of what it is to describe social action, both as lay person and social scientific observer, and resulted in the development of a major branch of sociological inquiry looking at the social world in a radically different way.[9]

A similar pattern is discernible with respect to the method known as participant observation which, among other things, claimed that many of the orthodox methods of social research failed properly to investigate the 'stuff' of social life.[10] To repeat the point: methods should not be regarded as atheoretical tools which do their job independently of any other consideration than their own elegance. They do their job because of other justifications which serve to underpin them. These justifications we earlier referred to as the instrumental and the theoretical presupposition of the method, and though the distinction between the two kinds of presuppositions is not a firm one it is worth maintaining for the following reason. As the pattern we iterated earlier illustrates, there is a period when methods do come to be seen as merely technical instruments beyond, as it were, proper theoretical debate. When a method does become fashionable in this way it tends to be used to crack each and every research problem irrespective of whether, in more sober times, it is appropriate for the particular project at hand. The theoretical and instrumental underpinnings tend to be forgotten until inconsistencies arise between the instrumental presuppositions and those embodied in theory. Inconsistencies which, when articulated, may become the basis for changes in the body of knowledge that constitute the discipline. The choice of methods of research, then, should not be based on technical criteria alone. An appreciation of their intellectual context of use, a changing context at that, is essential to evaluating their purpose and their power as instruments of research.

One could be forgiven for thinking that all that has just been said unduly complicates a topic which, in our experience, is for most students of sociology onerous and dull. As if mastery of the technical issues were not enough, we are suggesting that these be related to other matters broader in scope and, if anything, less capable of resolution. This would, we feel, be an unwarranted ground for pessimism. The study of methods should not be approached as our generation learned their tables, that is, by rote and endless repetition. A craftsman uses tools to ends of his own and finds pleasure in adapting his tools to all kinds of creative purposes. In this book what we hope to do is approach techniques of data selection in this spirit. We shall raise questions about methods which require consideration of their presuppositions, both what we have called 'instrumental' and 'theoretical', in the hope that students may begin to see methods as central to the theoretical concerns of the discipline of sociology and not some more or less useful adjunct.

Given the limits of this volume we have decided to select three aspects of data collection for detailed consideration rather than try to cover all the possible methods available to social scientists and run the risk of treating them too superficially. We do not discuss in any detail data collection techniques such as content analysis, life histories, the use of documents, the collection and use of official statistics, laboratory experiments, and so forth. The ones we have selected represent the methods in commonest use and, in addition, illustrate some of the wider concerns we have talked about in this chapter. Some of these wider concerns are discussed in Chapter 2 where we deal in more detail with questions and issues raised only briefly in this. Chapter 3 is a discussion of the sample survey and some of the problems arising from this method of organising the collection of sociological data. Here we identify the major types of survey and relate them to their historical intellectual context. Chapter 4 deals with a method commonly used in conjunction with the survey, namely, the interview. This method and that dealt with in Chapter 5, participant observation, are occasions when the researcher encounters the source of social science data: the member of society. Both are very much methods involving social encounters between the researcher, or usually an assistant, and the subject of the research, namely, to use an unsociological expression, people. Both methods, as we shall see, depend heavily upon theories of social encounters which, in their turn, are incorporated into what we can call the design of the method and its aims of eliciting data of a particular kind. However, though each of these methods share this quality, they do involve rather different conceptions about the nature of social encounters, indeed of social life itself, and, once again, we shall be forced to examine the presuppositions upon which they are based.

The final chapter (Ch. 6) presents a résumé of the various arguments raised in the book and hazards a few guesses about the proper relationship of methods and data collection to the wider sociological enterprise.

2

DATA AND SOCIAL THEORY

To put it very simply, social science is concerned with the explanation of human behaviour. Data of some kind will play an important role in such explanations, and to this end social scientists have devised methods for the systematic collection of data.

But understanding data collection in social science is not as simple as this bald account would suggest. As soon as we look at what social scientists actually do or what they claim they do, it becomes clear that there are a host of differences between them on some very basic issues. There are, to mention but a few, differences concerning the way human behaviour itself should be conceived, the way explanations should be arrived at and what they are, and what role data play in the social scientific enterprise. Many of these issues are philosophical in nature, and while it will not be possible to treat them all adequately some general discussion of them may help to clarify matters and point out to the reader the distinctive features of the approach being used here.[1]

It is possible to distinguish, if rather grossly, between two contrasting positions regarding the nature of theory and its relationship to data. Both agree that it is theories which do the job of explanation, but disagree in their conception both of theory itself and the relationship it has to data. The first view we may term the 'empiricist' and it derives from empiricist philosophies of science; a tradition which reaches back at least as far as Aristotle and runs through more recent figures as Locke, Hume, J.S. Mill, and the Logical Positivists. The second view owes rather more to a rationalistic philosophical tradition whose key figures include Plato, Descartes, and the great philosophical system builders Leibniz and Hegel.[2]

The 'empiricist' view sought the foundations of human knowledge in indubitable experience of the external world. The task of science was to formulate procedures whereby this external world could be accurately described, measured, and otherwise charted with certitude. Pride of place in this activity was given to systematic empirical investigation, and considerable effort and attention given to the development of methods of doing just this. Many of the methods of investigation used in the social sciences owe much to this spirit. For our purposes what is important is the emphasis on the collection of 'hard' facts about some subject, whatever it might be. The theoretical task, and in a significant sense secondary to the activity of collecting facts, was to link these together in some causal scheme. J. S. Mill, for example, proposed certain 'canons', or principles, by which the causal relationships could be determined. One of these was the 'method of agreement' which stated that if two or more instances of a phenomenon have only one element in common then this is the cause (or the effect) of the phenomenon in question. Similarly, his principle of 'concomitant variation' proposed that whatever phenomenon varies in any manner whenever another phenomenon varies, is either the cause or the effect of that phenomenon; a principle more familiarly known to us as correlation.[3] Through using these and other principles, the facts were ordered in terms of causal patterns. The theoretical resultant was a series of generalisations describing the causal association between the phenomena discovered.

For immediate purposes what is important about this and similar procedures is that the theoretical generalisation is induced from data systematically gathered. In other words, theory is subsequent to the collection of data or facts about the world. We shall see in later chapters how this conception infused many of the early exponents of the survey, to mention but one example. They saw their task as collecting facts about a population they were studying. For them the survey method embodied the scientific method since it sought factual knowledge out of which empirically based generalisations could be formulated. We can see it, too, in contemporary surveys which make use of various kinds of inductive statistics to effect generalisations from samples to populations. To some extent, though less so than in the case of the early surveyors, this empiricist spirit informed the early proponents of participant observation. They argued, and some still do, that in order fully to grasp how social situations are created and managed by social actors, social investigators need a full and rich repertoire of data gained by immersing themselves in the social worlds they are studying. Only then could theoretical speculation take place. Although they did differ markedly in the kind of data it was thought necessary to collect, both the early surveyors and some advocates of participant observation shared a similar view of the relationship between theory and data.

It should be no surprise that the view we have just summarised, though commonsensically plausible, came up against a number of philosophical difficulties. Moreover, although it retained some prima facie plausibility as an account of natural science, when transposed to the study of human social life other difficulties became transparent. One of the more important of the general philosophical problems was the empirical interpretation of scientific generalisations and theory. Laws in science, so it was argued, were of the logical form 'All A's are B's', yet it was in principle impossible to investigate empirically all A's, whatever they might be.[4] Empirical study always deals with a sample of phenomena, never a fully enumerated population. Even natural scientists experiment upon particular elements, chemical compounds, organisms, or whatever; never with all the instances of a particular element, chemical, or organism that have existed, do exist, or will exist. Accordingly, it appeared that law-like generalisations were always formulated by means of an inductive procedure whereby the sample investigated stood as surrogate for the total population. Unfortunately, this inductive procedure could not, logically speaking, underpin determinate laws, as they thought natural science had succeeded in discovering, but only probabilistic ones.

The second of the views we have distinguished, the 'rationalistic' one, derives from a claim that the route to indubitable knowledge is not through experience of the external world, but through logical principles which were beyond reasonable philosophical doubt. Whereas for the empiricists the criteria of knowledge were to be found in the practice of empirical science, for the rationalists the appropriate models were those of logic and mathematics. Here the logical principle involved is deduction. Theories are deductive systems of thought in which 'facts' are deduced from higher-order principles in a systematic, logical fashion, much as geometricians effect a proof by showing how the conclusion logically follows from one or two general premises or postulates. In this way, theory, or the general explanatory principles, assume a much greater importance than in the empiricist tradition.

As accounts of scientific procedure it was the empiricist one which became predominant though not without modification. Indeed, the orthodox account of social scientific practice these days represents a somwhat unequal marriage of the two positions we have just outlined. The empiricist account of theories has largely been discredited, but not the important stress it lays upon systematic methods of empirical investigation. The principle of deduction is incorporated by seeing empirical investigation as primarily concerned not simply with 'discovering facts' but with testing theories. The model here, called the 'hypothetico-deductive model', argues that general theories, couched in a universal form, while not logically provable, can be disproved by one counter instance.[5] Accordingly, using the general statements of the theory as premises in a deductive argument, along with statements describing the conditions under which the test is to be carried out, a testable conclusion can be deduced and compared with empirical evidence. If the evidence and the conclusion do not match, the theory is falsified; if they do match, then the researcher has some evidence for the theory and the next task is to examine its range of applicability. We shall see something of this in connection with the later developments in survey research design.

Even though this conception of the aim of science incorporates rationalistic elements, it does retain an emphasis on the methodical collection of data. Moreover, it stresses the importance of accurate measurement in order that theories may be tested more precisely and their range more accurately gauged. Systematic research methods are the means of linking theory to the empirical world. Associated with this is a tendency to see methods as theoretically neutral tools: a view, as we hope to show, that is both misleading and defective. Furthermore, in neither the empiricist nor the hybrid account we have just described was much interest expressed in the nature and origin of theory. The origin of theory was seen as a matter of conjecture or imagination, certainly beyond the scope of scientific concern. Of much greater importance was the responsiveness of the theory, whatever its content and origins, to scientific test. This was the important, the crucial, criterion. Although theories could never be conclusively proved, empirical research could falsify them and so help rule out the many alternative and often competing theories.[6] Thus, the product of conjecture and imagination could be tidied up and disciplined by empirical research.

More recent philosophies of social science have begun to take this model to task.[7] But, for our purposes, what is important to note at this stage is the view of methods as atheoretical tools; ways of confronting theory with the 'facts' of the external world. Unfortunately, in the context of social science this view is not so easily maintained, for reasons which we have already indicated in Chapter 1 and will discuss in further detail in succeeding chapters.

Methodological approaches to social science emerge, develop, and, of course, fade away. In this respect two factors are important to note. First of all, an approach to social science emerges in a particular social context marked, among other things, by especially influential social groups and particularly authoritative doctrines. Both of these will inevitably influence the character of social research in various ways.[8] Second, an approach to social science is developed *by* a social group. The perceptions that a research community develops will be influenced by a whole set of factors, none more potent than the ideas and practices that have been used previously, as well as those which are seen to yield or not to yield advances in understanding. Such factors as these underlie the processes of development outlined at the end of Chapter 1. There is, in other words, an important social dimension necessary to the understanding of both the development of methods and methodology and the kind of presuppositions on which they are based.

Our approach involves substantially discarding the view which sees methods as tools in favour of one which sees them as an integral part of social science itself. Especially important in this regard is what we term the 'theoretical context of method'; that is, the intellectual justifications offered for the uses to which they are put. We have already mentioned in Chapter 1 two kinds of justificatory presuppositions, the instrumental and the theoretical, and have just suggested that these are related in some complex way to the social context in which methods are used. In the remainder of this chapter we will develop this point of view in connection with some examples of data and research methods, and contrast it with what we might term the 'orthodox stance' towards methods of data collection.

The orthodox view sees methods of research more or less as tools and there are two closely related variants of this worth mentioning. The first is the 'nature of the problem' view, according to which there are methods ready and waiting for any research occasion. Research is simply a matter of defining, relatively explicitly, the nature of our problem in order to undertake appropriate research. All a researcher has to do is look on the shelf containing methods of research and select the appropriate one for his research problem. The second and related variant, which is scarcely more defensible, is the 'nature of the method' approach, which suggests that there are only certain limited potentialities in particular methods and, to this extent we must recognise that certain methods can discover only certain things. To some degree this is true, but the reasons for it are complex.

Both of these variants contain kernels of truth about the nature of research methods. But the major fault we find with them is that they present a view in which theoretical considerations are too divorced from technical ones. While it is often the case that methods are treated as if they were tools in a tool box ready and waiting to be used for their appropriate job, it is vitally important that any aspiring methodologist does not take this too seriously, but tries to understand the kind of presupposition underpinning methods we have been talking about.

One consequence of the 'tool-box' view is a tendency to use data generically without too much regard for the theoretical issues involved in their production. This 'tool-box' view can be briefly summarised as follows. There are 'facts' in the world, recorded in various ways, and all a researcher has to do is gather those relevant to the problem at hand. It matters little whether the 'facts' or the 'data' are produced by a questionnaire survey, found in a document, or the result of observation. Admittedly, there may be problems of a technical nature, but these are treated as of little theoretical moment.

However, by contrast, some research methods and the data they generate, develop within a particular theoretical tradition or approach. These represent theory-specific uses of a method. The distinction between generic and theory-specific methods is important though often overlooked by methodologists. It is important because theory-specific methods are at their most effective when used within their appropriate theoretical context. Outside of the appropriate theoretical context, theory-specific methods can be more of a liability than an asset. Such a user is likely to draw conclusions from the data which are not warranted by the theoretical presuppositions of the method. The line between generic and theory-specific data and methods is not always easy to draw and is a moving one as we shall see. Our primary interest in this book is with two classical social science methods; surveys carried out with interviewing, and participant observation, both of which have been put to theory-specific uses. Although these methods are often taught as if they were exclusively generic, in fact this is not so. The method of participant observation, for example, was mostly developed within the symbolic interactionist approach to sociology, and has been refined almost exclusively by researchers adopting this framework. It has been in the main theory-specific. By contrast, the survey was developed as a generic method for use to practical ends. Only subsequently was it rendered more theory-specific, and has passed through several theory-specific types. In other words, methods have a habit of crossing the distinction between generic and theory-specific in response to developments within the social science disciplines.

We have come a long way in this discussion without saying anything about what actually count as data in the social sciences, apart from indicating that they will concern human behaviour and be used in the explanation of that behaviour. There are problems to do with trying to stipulate precisely the character of such data since, as has already been suggested, it is often the case that different theoretical schools within the social sciences have rather different views about the nature of human behaviour, the way it is to be studied and hence, also to have different conceptions of what data are. Some, indeed, would say that the very term 'data' itself limits the possible options in this respect by implying that there are special kinds or orders of phenomena which qualify for special consideration to the exclusion of other phenomena. For the behaviourists only overt behaviour was deemed to be appropriate data for psychological research. This had the intended effect of ruling out of court references to innate and subjective mental states or the meaning attributed to objects, events, or persons by actors. In a similar fashion, Durkheim sought to establish the scientific credentials of sociology by arguing that it should be concerned with its own special order of 'facts': that is, those social events and processes which possessed the qualities of externality, and endowed with the power of constraint; examples of such 'social facts' being language, law, custom, economic and political organisations, and so on. In other words, in both these cases only certain phenomena would qualify as data.[9]

In the social sciences the things that are considered as data range from very narrowly conceived bodily behaviour, such as eye movements, to complex packages of motives and attitudes, to descriptions of aggregates of populations of people, and so on. That these and other things are taken as data in particular research projects is determined not only, or even mainly, by the subject-matter of the research, for example, friendship group formation, marriage choice, consumer expenditures, revolutions, or whatever, but also by the theory and presuppositions in which the study is formulated. What count as data will be determined by the theory involved in the formulation of the research project, and not from common-sense ideas about the nature of the topic. As we have said before, in a strict sense, sociology, or any social science for that matter, does not study people as we know them in our day-to-day lives, but selected aspects of their lives, loves, hates, and other doings. Moreover, each approach within the various social sciences often contains different conceptions, different selections from the lives, relationships, and beliefs of people.

This is one of the basic difficulties in the way of producing a neat definition of data. If, as we are arguing, methods are, or should be, an extension of theory, there would seem to be no theory-neutral language by which we can compare different methods. Also, different things qualify for consideration as data. It also complicates the task of exposition in that it makes direct comparison of methods difficult, if not impossible. This issue is a vexing one to which we shall return, but it is worth considering in some detail here through the notion of 'operational definitions', and so illustrate some of the problems involved. Earlier in this chapter we remarked that the prevailing view of methods is to see them as alternative ways of confronting theory with the facts of the world. Theories are, at least in principle, deductively organised sets of propositions and assumptions which, at some point, generate empirical statements capable of being true or false as judged by the facts of the world. This means that at least some of the statements in the theory should be empirically translatable; that is, have meaning in terms of things in the world which are, in some form, observable. Thus, if we are testing some predictions of structural-functional theory, a researcher would need to define at least some of the expressions used in the theory in terms of observables. What, for example, is to be taken as indicative of 'integration', of 'values', of 'moral restraints', and so on. Solutions to these kinds of problems will obviously emerge from elaborations of the theory itself, while others may require more ingenuity. Suppose, to use another example, that the concept of 'alienation' looms large in some theory a researcher wishes to test or examine further. If the concept requires to be given empirical meaning then the researcher will have to decide what kind of facts will be indicative of this concept. As we have already suggested, this is not a matter of the researcher's personal whim since, likely as not, he, or she, will be able to draw upon authoritative tradition.[10] In the case of the concept 'alienation', one tradition argues that it refers to a state of mind, one that it expresses withdrawal from or disenchantment with the life one leads. Accordingly, the researcher

might decide that the most effective way of measuring this state
of mind is through an attitude scale consisting of a series of
statements judged to express 'alienation', and to which subjects
have to respond in terms of degrees of agreement and disagreement. An example of such a statement might be, 'For me life
simply has no meaning', or 'Even when I am enjoying myself I
often feel that I don't belong'. A scale of this kind will normally
consist of a number of such statements. But the point is that in
this example the scale constitutes an empirical index for the
theoretical concept 'alienation'. If you like, the scale effects a
translation between two languages: a theoretical one, in which
the meaning of the expressions is largely determined by their
relationship to each other, and an empirical one in which meaning is a matter of reference to facts in the empirical world. In
short, the scale becomes an 'operational definition' of a theoretical concept.

As one might expect, the relationship between these 'operational definitions' and the theoretical concepts they are supposed
to index has been a matter of much debate. Theoretical concepts
are, by their nature, much wider in their meaning than operational definitions. To refer back to the example above, the
statements selected by the researcher could not exhaust all the
possible statements that could be used. A researcher has prac-
ticalities to take into account. It may be, for example, that an
attitude scale, for whatever reason, could not be used as an
index. In this case other measures would have to serve as an
index of 'alienation', say, for example, the extent of participation
in friendship groups, voluntary associations, and so forth. But,
then, what is the relationship between the first index and the
second? Both are intended to measure the same theoretical concept, but do they?

The answer to these questions is as much a theoretical one as
it is a methodological one. The doctrine of operationalism took a
particular and rather extreme view of this issue by arguing that
the meaning of a concept consisted in the operations required to
measure it. Thus, strictly interpreted, the meaning of the concept 'alienation' is the attitude scale used to measure it. Of
course, the implication of this is that a different measure is also a
different concept. This is hardly a satisfactory conclusion for

those who wished to argue that different measures are not different concepts but simply indices of other aspects of the same overall theoretical concept. Once again we see how theoretical considerations are deeply embedded in methods of research.

Both of the research strategies which will be examined in the following chapters have been used in the service of more than one theory or approach although, because of the close association of the method with symbolic interactionism, participant observation has been less prone to indiscriminate use. None the less, there have been occasions when this method has been used for theoretical purposes other than those for which it was originally devised. Nor is this unusual as the growing use of secondary data suggests.

We have already remarked in the introduction that data collection is increasingly prevalent in all kinds of organisations. The various branches of the state in modern societies are important in this respect. Such is the cost of large-scale research these days that it is a standing temptation to tap the rich reservoirs of data collected by others for other purposes. Hence, it is hardly surprising that use of other people's data as material to work with, particularly the official statistics compiled by government departments, has a long history.

Once again, there are different ways in which such data are used, but all share the object of analysing the data anew, using them for a different purpose than that for which they were originally intended. The normal use of this kind of data involves showing that the conclusions originally drawn are unwarranted or even incorrect and, perhaps, that contrary conclusions are indicated. However, a rather more theoretically informed use of secondary data is possible as in the following classic example. Durkheim made use of officially collected data relating to suicides in Europe, particularly in France, to demonstrate the validity of his theories of the social causation of suicidal behaviour: an object for which the statistics were definitely not originally intended.[11]

As to whether Durkheim was justified in using the data in the way that he did, or whether the data on suicide rates can be regarded as supporting his theories, is a very important issue and has been the focus of one of the most interesting debates in the methodological literature of recent years. If the argument advanced in Chapter 1 is correct, there is some point to this debate. What Durkheim did was to transform or recontextualise the data, the official statistics, produced by officials for their own administrative purposes, and relate them to his theoretical concerns. Others, notably Cicourel and Douglas, have challenged the assumptions Durkheim made about the nature of official statistics and in so doing made important elaborations in sociological theory: elaborations which have had profound methodological consequences.[12]

For our purposes what is important here is the way in which what we might call, somewhat misleadingly, the 'raw data' are transformed by placing them in a different theoretical perspective. With reference to suicide statistics, Durkheim did this first of all by transforming the rates compiled by officials in pursuance of their routine duties from a simple factual registration of certain types of death to indicators of a 'suicidogenic current' caused by various states of the society itself. Much later the same 'raw data', as it were, were transformed yet again in response to defects felt to be inherent in Durkheim's work, and instead seen to be the resultant of various kinds of social actors, especially but not only officials, using conventional meanings to make sense of and to construct their social worlds.[13] This illustrates, once again, how data are intimately responsive to theory and the other kinds of presuppositions we have mentioned.

To come back to a method we shall be discussing more fully in Chapter 3, we can see much the same sort of development with respect to the survey method. The social survey method was used originally to discover what were regarded as facts about the population of a particular society; facts especially to do with income and personal expenditure. This was later widened into seeking from respondents, again in sufficient numbers to be indicative of the whole society, facts of other sorts, such as marital status, housing, level of education, and leisure use. Thus, the accounts offered by respondents of their experience and behaviour were taken, quite reasonably it was felt at the time, as indicative of a fairly static social fabric called the 'social structure'.[14]

The theory, if such it can be called, which underwrote this use of the survey, was a 'naïve empiricist structuralism', according to which the structure of society is susceptible to factual observation and description. Finding out 'facts' about the people who constitute the population was the essence of scientific investigation. Significantly for us, the use of interviews and mass surveys as methods of data collection involved the notion that the accounts respondents offered of their condition and experiences were as good as direct observation of those respondents themselves. This is the closest social science has come to pure 'empiricism', or, as it is sometimes disparagingly referred to, 'vulgar fact gathering'. Yet it is important to note that theoretical interpretation, even if unacknowledged, was involved. For example, taking the answer given by a respondent to a question as equivalent to observation of the event to which it refers, was an assumption upon which the method rested. Indeed, this was the basic reason underlying the insistence of the early survey users that questions be restricted to those capable of unambiguous factual reply. Such assumptions commit the user of the method to various instrumental theories about the relationship of types of question to types of answer, the effect or, to be more accurate, the non-effect, of the contexts in which questions are asked, and so on. It also commits the user to wider theoretical positions such as the 'factual' nature of the social structure, its objectivity, and so on. As we shall see in the next chapter, many of these early instrumental and other theoretical conceptions underpinning the survey and the interview have proved less than durable.

Certainly, modern sociological uses of the survey method have discarded what are now regarded as rather naïve methodological assumptions of the early survey. In the 1940s and 1950s in the United States, data produced by the survey were put to a different use. It was argued, to put the matter briefly, that social acts were essentially motivated behaviour and could only be properly explained if understood in terms of these underlying dispositions to act. So, data generated from surveys were used to infer a 'latent structure' of respondent attitudes and motivations.[15] Rather than seeing responses to questions as simple indicators of 'factual' events, these theorists saw them as data from which it was possible to infer knowledge about the dispositional and motivational contents of respondents' minds. These, in their turn, were seen as indispensable for the explanation of actual behaviour. In a very real sense, although answers to questions are being elicited in both approaches, the data that result are fundamentally different. Not only do the questions themselves differ fundamentally – in this one asking for purely 'factual' information, in the others stating or asking about an opinion or a belief – the answers themselves are used in different ways. For the early empiricists, the answers taken in conjunction with other facts about the social structure add up to a description of a particular society. For the latent structure analysts, the answers index deeper personality factors, and when appropriately processed can reveal a respondent's psycho-social orientation which can then be used to explain his or her social action.

The kind of theory invoked by latent structure analysis was basically socio-psychological and cultural. The argument runs that different components of personality are built up in particular individuals as a consequence of participating in particular cultures. Hence, the aim of their analysis of attitudes was to reveal the hidden patterns typically sedimented in particular social contexts. Having a particular view about the origin of personality, as well as the structures they might find, these survey users were not nearly so preoccupied with representative samples of the whole society, but tended to produce analyses of the data showing close associations between sets of attitudes and correlations between these and other social behaviour.

What should be clear by now is that data, whatever else they may consist in, have to be 'read' through theoretically informed eyes to exist as data at all. Even the generic kinds of data we mentioned earlier are theoretically contextualised, albeit in an often crude but more usually implicit fashion. Another way of putting this general point is to say that the world only exists as data through interpretations that are placed upon it. It should also be clear that this fact presents social science with rather special problems to do with evaluating theories by means of data. If, as we have strongly suggested, the character of data has much to do with the theoretical presuppositions which underlie their production, how can it be said that the theories are tested by means of exposure, in some fashion, to empirical data? Indeed, if we examine social scientific practice at all closely we can often see how substantially the same data can be used to support or discredit very different, even contrary, theories. As we pointed out earlier, the generic use of data and methods should not make this too surprising an observation. Some years ago the major theoretical dispute in sociology was between functionalism and conflict theories, each, in a sense, making use of the same 'facts' to support its own case and discredit that of the other. Another way of making this point is to say that many social science theories are inexactly determined by the facts and as such seem to have more in common with moral and political positions than they have with natural scientific theories.[16] In other words, despite the prevalent support given to the 'hypothetico-deductive model' as an account of the relationship between theory and data, many of the disputes in social science are not about theories in this sense but about *approaches* to social science and about the way in which the 'facts' of the social world are to be fundamentally interpreted; in short, about ways in which the social world should be read.[17] Once again we come up against the 'complicated machinery' behind the business end that is research methods. In this region there are, unfortunately (or fortunately, depending on one's morale) no easy answers.

The foregoing discussion has tried to make the point that research methods cannot stand in isolation from the profound theoretical issues which dominate the social sciences. While problems of method may be reduced to purely technical issues, such as: how many people shall we interview?; how long shall we observe the group?; what is an acceptable chi-square value?; and so on, little of this will cast any light on the crucial issues of method, namely, what shall we study? What we study follows from the theoretical rather than the technical or the practical. In the chapters which follow we hope to show that methods are not, and cannot be, selected according to the qualities of the data they yield alone. The richness of the data sought by participant observation methods, for example, and the objective and representative data sought by the survey are not, by themselves, virtues. The point is that they are qualities deliberately sought because some theoretical schema or approach requires them.

So far we have been raising rather large issues in an abstracted fashion which, it is hoped, will become clear as they are addressed and filled out during discussion of specific methods of data collection. Finally, in this chapter we want to return to the fundamental source of social science data and the ultimate object of social scientific explanation, namely, social actors or, as they are better known, people. Social science, it should not need pointing out, is concerned to understand, explain if you will, the social origins, context, and consequences of what the members of society do, the relationships they form, what they believe in, think about, pray to, fight about, collaborate about, discover, create, and so on. Though the various social sciences, and within each discipline, differ, often violently, as to how this understanding should be achieved they do at least share this general aim. To this extent, then, they also share a common source of data, namely, what members of society have produced, and are producing in the way of artefacts, social groups, institutions, documents of various kinds, systems of conflict and co-operation, and, of course, society itself. Very generally, we can analyse what this source of data produces into the following components: elements which research methods use in some form or another, some emphasising one at the expense of others, some using one as evidence of others, and so on, but each element constituting the raw material of more complex data productions. The first element consists in what people do, their acts, or their behaviour. The second are the thoughts, aspirations, beliefs, values, motives, etc. that people hold: in other words, internal mental states which may or may not be associated with particular acts or behaviour. Third is their speech, either verbal or written, which accompany actions, report on them, or state such things as values, beliefs, opinions, and other 'internal' subjective states. With respect to each of these elements there are widely differing interpretations as to their nature and which have profound methodological consequences. However, the conventional mode of social scientific explanation sees these as analytically separate elements representing, as it were, different orders of phenomena and data. On this view, one of the more important problems of methods is to relate these various elements in systematic ways. Thus, the interview is often used to inquire into the beliefs and values of a particular group in society on the supposition that these are crucial to the explanation of what members of the group do. This could arise in researching into, for example, the voting behaviour or other political preferences of white collar workers, or the differential rates of absenteeism among groups of workers within an industry. The beliefs, the internally and subjectively held beliefs, influencing, at least in part, the behaviour in which members of these groups engage and which distinguishes them from other groups who hold different beliefs.[18] The methodological problem, in the conventional mode of social scientific methodology, arises because beliefs, attitudes, values, and other so-called subjective states, cannot be directly inspected. Accordingly, they have to be inferred, usually through some form of verbal behaviour such as the responses to attitude scales or other kinds of questionnaire items. In its turn this leads on to problems to do with the extent to which, and the conditions under which, respondents accurately report their beliefs, etc. and, ultimately, to the extensive and impressive technology of interview and attitude measurement.

Some of these issues we shall deal with more fully in the chapter on the interview. But the point we want to make for immediate purposes has to do with the way in which methodological problems arise from particular conceptions of the 'order of things'. In other conceptions problems of this particular kind do not arise.[19] An alternative philosophy of science, for example, argues that the distinctions noted above are by no means clear and that behaviour cannot be identified in isolation from speech and so-called 'internal' mental states. It denies, in other words, the intelligibility of the notion of a language to describe behaviour neutrally which is, at the same time, socially and sociologically informative. In this case, the elements we have identified above are not, logically speaking, analytically independent.

On top of all this there is a further theme to do with the collective nature of social life. All the social sciences are predicated on the notion that individuals are not isolated like so many Robinson Crusoes but are related to others in complex ways. It is these relationships, we could say, which form the focus of interest of the social sciences. Human beings form economic relationships of many kinds with each other, involve themselves in political relationships, live within many kinds of groups and so on. As Durkheim and others tried to demonstate, these relationships seem to have an independent existence over and above the individuals who compose them. Individuals live and die, but economic systems, political systems, society itself, show a durability that goes beyond the lifespan of any one individual. The methodological problem arises because, it can be argued, all we can observe and gather data from, are individuals. Only individuals can fill out questionnaires, be interviewed, respond to attitude scales, be observed within task groups, and so on, and yet these data are often used as evidence for, or descriptions of, these supraindividual phenomena to which we have just referred. Accordingly, methodology, but mainly theory, needs some conceptualisation as to how this may be achieved, and as we shall see in Chapter 3 efforts to overcome the excessive 'individualism' of the method are being made.

There are many problems here and we cannot hope to deal with them all adequately, not simply because of the limitations of space in a short book of this kind, but, more importantly, because many of these are, as yet, problems to which there are no satisfactory answers, even though some new directions are becoming visible, as we will try to show throughout the following discussion. What we hope we have shown in a general way so far is the vital link between theory and method which is so essential to a full understanding of something as prosaic as methods of data collection. In Chapter 3 we deal with the first of the substantive methods, the survey, and intend to flesh out some of the points we have raised in this chapter.

3

SOCIAL SURVEYS

Most of us in industrialised societies are familiar with social surveys of one type or another. Few of us would be too surprised to find an interviewer on our doorstep asking us to give a few moments of our time to answer one or two questions on our voting habits, which TV programmes we watch, whether our socks are washed in Daz or Bold, or whatever. Some of us may even have taken part in an academic survey. Certainly all of us will, or will already have at some time, take part in the national census. All of which means that most people will have an intuitive grasp of what social surveys are about: they are concerned with finding out what views people hold about particular events or things and, of course, with collecting other kinds of information from them. In this chapter we shall be considering the theoretical ideas which have, and still do, inform social surveys, their origins and their applications. As the above introductory remarks suggest, the experience most people have with social surveys is through an interview. For the sake of convenience this will be considered in Chapter 4, even though it is essential to remember that the data collected through social surveys are almost exclusively obtained by means of an interview.

We shall consider four types of survey. The first is the social survey which aims at eliciting general facts about the condition and the organisation of whole societies. This was the first kind of social survey to be seriously used in this country, and its importance, as we argue here, is due to historical and political factors. What this approach has done is provide procedures for surveying large numbers of people at minimum cost, and a series of guides for eliciting 'factual' information from respondents in an interview situation. We shall call it for convenience the 'factual' survey. The factual survey may be contrasted with 'attitude surveying,' which aims at producing an accurate picture of the attitudes people hold as a guide to their likely behaviour. This was the first kind of survey to be seriously undertaken in the USA, and its importance can similarly be attributed to economic and social factors peculiar to the USA at that stage of its history. This approach has bequeathed us the procedures known as the quota sample and the attitude questionnaire. The main aim of both these types of survey was to effect as accurate as possible a description of the social structure, as it was called, or, as in the case of the attitude survey, the current state of public opinion. By contrast, the third and fourth types we identify were more concerned with explanation and theory-testing than with description. The 'social psychological survey', for example, uses survey design and questionnaires to investigate personality via various kinds of attitude-measurement techniques. Finally, there is the survey concerned with eliciting from respondents information designed to test some theoretical explanation, and which we shall call, for convenience, the 'explanatory survey.'

In an important way, the 'factual survey' and the 'attitude survey' were designed to achieve practical rather than theoretical ends. The interests which stimulated their innovation and guided their use were primarily political as distinct from purely academically theoretical. It was assumed that if reliable knowledge about the state of society was to be attained then the whole population of that society must be investigated. This was certainly the view behind the first major social surveys of income and consumption carried out in this country by Booth in London and Rowntree in York.[1] It was also assumed by the early attitude surveys of public opinion in the United States, as we shall see. Though Booth and Rowntree were wealthy industrialists, it was principally considerations of cost which led to them limiting themselves to the study of particular areas. What seems fairly clear is that had it been possible to study the whole country relatively cheaply and in sufficient detail they would probably have done so.[2]

So, two key assumptions governed the early social surveys used in this country and the opinion surveys developed in the

United States. First, the greater the absolute size of the population under study and the closer it approximates to the total population of the country, the better. Second, the higher the proportion of this population which can be contacted the better. Developments in sampling statistics weakened the force of both these assumptions quite early in this country. Reliable generalisations could be made about the whole population of a society based on the systematic use of sampling techniques. The whole population was still the focus of interest, though sampling techniques enabled it to be studied economically through a population sample that was considerably less in number than the whole. But the aim to study the whole population determined the scope and character of these two types of survey and, in so doing, encouraged the search for ways of doing this economically which, as we have said, led to innovations in the applications of statistical theory.

The early 'factual' social surveys

Given the interests of the early social surveyors in investigating whole populations we must include among the forerunners of the social survey the censuses of pre-modern times. The two best known of these are the one undertaken by Augustus Caesar, which affected the circumstances of the birth of Christ, and the Domesday Survey compiled at the instigation of William I. Both of these were attempts by an occupying power to extend its control over a subject population. Data in each of these cases were sought by the central administration of the dominating power for taxation and other purposes so that money and other forms of tribute could be more effectively extracted, and the rewards for loyal service allocated. It was this legacy of coercive intent which encouraged resistance to attempts to introduce a census in this country until the beginning of the last century.[3]

By the time the first censuses were taken in Britain much had changed in the structure of society and the nature of the state. By 1801, not only had the conflicts between monarch and nobility over the extraction and use of rents and taxes largely passed away, but the industrial revolution was well advanced, establishing the growing political ascendancy of the industrialist over both monarchy and aristocracy. The character of the state had changed decisively from the coercive apparatus of monarchical power to the increasingly bureaucratic (but determinedly *laissez-faire*) administration of the first capitalist industrial nation. Indeed, the concepts developed by the classical political economists, such as Smith, Ricardo, and Malthus, influenced the categories used in the first British censuses.[4] Since then the assumptions underpinning, and the meaning attributed to, census data have changed a good deal. Nowadays the census does not seek information about the numbers of people obtaining support from different factors of production but has extended its range into a whole gamut of policy-related matters such as housing, education, and income as well as occupation. The census has also become an important instrument, among a range of similar investigative procedures, in the administration of the welfare state.

This development of the census (and other official data collection practices) as an integral part of the welfare state is a comparatively recent development in this country. Much of the early social survey work was concerned with revealing the need for social welfare provision along the lines now embodied in the modern welfare state. Also, the census was slow to be influenced by the techniques of survey methods, both in the use of sample designs and in the search for more appropriate data. A biographer has said of A. L. Bowley, the man who above all others took up the mantle of Booth and Rowntree in the early part of this century, that: '... it was unfortunately not the custom in Bowley's day for the British Government to call outside experts. Undoubtedly British official statistics would have advanced more rapidly, particularly in the use of sampling techniques, if Bowley had had more to do with them.'[5]

Britain was comparatively slow in acquiring a welfare state in comparison with other countries, particularly Germany, and it is in the context of the struggle to achieve more adequate welfare provision that the early uses of the social surveys in this country must be understood.

The process of industrialisation not only began later in Germany than here, but that country also achieved spectacular economic success in a relatively short time. In the space of two decades Germany rapidly overtook Britain in industrial output. By the early years of the present century, and certainly well before the outbreak of the First World War, Germany was increasingly challenging Britain's dominance as the world's leading industrial and political power. That Germany had provided comprehensive state insurance for sickness, accident, disability and unemployment for its people from an early date was thought by some to be implicated in its phenomenal success. Also, the inability of Britain to sustain economic growth from 1870 or so onwards was partly explained by inadequate welfare provision. About this time a long depression hit the British economy, giving further impetus to the reappraisal of social and economic policy being undertaken at the time. Among other things we find at this time is the transformation of British liberal political thought from a straightforward advocacy of *laissez-faire* non-intervention to what has been called 'social liberalism'.[6] Social liberalism and allied doctrines, such as Fabian Socialism, provided important ingredients of the intellectual context in which the pioneering social survey work was carried out in this country. Social liberals like Booth and Rowntree and Fabians like Sydney and Beatrice Webb may have differed in their views on the extent and permanence of the provision of state welfare that they advocated, but they shared an interest in what they saw as the factual demonstration of the extent of poverty which existed at the time. For similar reasons they advocated the use of survey research which would show in considerable detail the actual extent of existing social conditions in a way that would be particularly difficult to disbelieve.

While it would be going too far to claim that social surveys such as these by themselves induced major political change in this country, in the circumstances in which they were used they powerfully augmented other forces of change by providing data on the state of society when so little was previously known. This can be illustrated by the early surveys of Booth and Rowntree. At the time the prevailing view of poverty was that it was primarily due to personal inadequacy, especially laziness and moral turpitude. This was convenient for the predominant political thinking of the period which held that intervention by the state in either the economy or the society was invidious, partisan, and, what is more, unnecessary. It was the scale of poverty revealed by the Booth and Rowntree surveys which shocked late Victorian sensibilities. Both surveys showed that for many people poverty was a way of life even when they were in gainful employment. This struck at the root of the idea that nobody need be poor if they conscientiously engaged in economic activity. As a result, the view came to be increasingly accepted that persistent (and unacceptable) inequality and want might be built into the economic system unless the state made key interventions along the lines of the German model. The shift towards a greater acceptance of this point of view marks the emergence of social from *laissez-faire* liberalism; a shift assisted in no small measure by the early poverty surveys.

If liberalism was a spent political force in this country by 1930, the kind of social survey to which it helped give rise was not. Sampling techniques, which will be described in the next section, were refined throughout the early decades of this century by A. L. Bowley, J. Hilton, and others. Such methods were increasingly copied and applied within the apparatus of the welfare state, and became an important element in its maintenance and extension.[7] Moser writes: 'By the middle of 1930s surveys were beginning to assume importance in the field of town planning and reconstruction ... .'[8]

By 1941 social surveys on the lines pioneered by Booth, Rowntree, and Bowley were fully incorporated within the welfare state, further impelled by the administrative and logistic needs of war, with the creation of the Government Social Survey in 1941 as an adjunct to the Central Statistical Office. This has more recently been combined into the Office of Population Censuses and Surveys. In modern times the social survey has changed from being an instrument used to demonstrate the desirability of centralised welfare administration to a central feature of its maintenance and support. Moser writes, very revealingly, of the Government Social Survey: 'The survey exists to collect data required for administration, not for party politics.'[9]

Incidentally, Moser himself, who identifies survey work very much with the tradition of national sample surveys, became Director of the Central Statistical Office, so prolonging the tradition of Booth and Rowntree.

While the ability of the social survey to provide a large-scale picture of prevailing social conditions is important, such surveys are not frequently undertaken today. To the extent that social research generally retained an interest in social reform it has been redirected in various ways. Among the new directions we can include research on the extent to which material deprivation exists among particular groups in society, the study of dimensions of inequality other than material, towards study of welfare institutions of the state itself, and so on. Where such studies make use of the survey method they tend to be smaller in scale and more analytic than descriptive, using samples drawn from relevant subgroups.

Contributions of the early surveys: probability sampling

We have remarked that the social and intellectual origins of the early surveys in this country gave them a particular emphasis. This may be summed up as the aims of generality and factuality. That is, the aim of describing the state of society by gathering hard facts about the conditions of life from as many people as possible: hard facts to do with income, expenditure, consumption, and so forth. Little interest was expressed in gathering facts about how people felt about the conditions under which they lived, or their hopes and fears of the future. Facts were to do with the material conditions of life, described as precisely as possible and counted as accurately as possible. In terms of the impulse for social reform which motivated many of these surveys, such facts, scientifically garnered, would be difficult to rebut by the opponents of reform.

Although in terms of later social science methodologies such an approach might seem naïve, it did leave an important legacy for social research and data collection, namely, sampling. The desire to survey the social conditions of the largest possible population proved difficult to execute economically, so methods were sought which would make the costs of such surveys more reasonable without, at the same time, significantly reducing the reliability of the data gathered. Sampling provided a means to do this.

Sampling techniques were adopted from statisticians working in the fields of biology and botany.[10] The statistical theories involved were designed to allow generalisations about a population to be made on the basis of the study of a sample of that population, within known margins of error. Thus, to give a simple enough example, a precise estimate of the average height of adult males in this country can be made on the basis of a sample of adult males chosen at random. Since the population of adult males in this country is many million, there are obvious savings to be made using this technique. It means that the population value of some characteristic, whether it be income, educational level, consumption pattern, voting intention, and so on, can be estimated, within a certain range of error, from the values found within a suitably drawn sample of that population.

While this is not the place to enter into a detailed exposition of the mathematics behind sampling theory, there are two questions worth considering: how large does a sample have to be for a given population? and, how can we be sure that it provides a basis for an accurate and reliable estimate of the population itself? Without going into statistical details, generally speaking the larger the population the smaller the proportion of individuals that need to be sampled. The ratio of sample to population is normally expressed as a fraction, known as the sampling fraction. In our example of estimating the height of adult males in Britain, the sampling fraction would be about 1/4000, whereas to estimate the same parameter in a population of 200, a sampling fraction of 1/4, or a sample size of 50, would be necessary; in other words, the sample in the latter case would have to be a greater proportion of the total than in the former.[11]

However, sample sizes cannot be decided independently of considerations of acceptable error since sampling cannot guarantee that it will provide the true population value: what it does offer is ways of calculating the probable size of the error in estimating that value. Probability has a very precise meaning here. It will be possible for a researcher to know, for example, that there is 99 per cent probability that the sample estimate falls within 3 per cent of the real value in the total population. By and large, larger samples will increase precision, the less likely they are to vary from the population value, and the more confident we can be that our estimate of the population value is within a given range of accuracy. For any chosen sample size there will be a calculable range of variation within which an estimate of the population value falls, and an associated probability that the estimate will fall within that range. For any sample size there will be an inverse relationship between these two: the smaller the range specified, the lower the probability of accuracy it will be possible to associate with it. Thus, for example, we may be 99 per cent sure that the true population value is within 3 per cent of an estimate, or 99.9 per cent sure that it falls within 10 per cent of the same estimate, or 95 per cent certain it falls within 1 per cent of the estimate.

There are no absolute standards in the calculations, merely conventional ones. Confidence limits of 95 per cent and 99 per cent are conventionally used in many statistical calculations, not only in descriptive studies of the sort we are examining here but also in more analytical studies of the kind we shall be considering later in this chapter. In choosing a sample size, therefore, not only considerations of accuracy enter, but of conventionally acceptable limits as well.

In order to take advantage of the statistical principles which allow generalisations of the kind we have been describing, it is essential that sampling be carried out in a random manner. Randomness, which has a very precise meaning in this context, is necessary in order to ensure that the estimate of the population value which is sought is not biased. What it means is that every individual comprising the population of interest should have an equal chance of being selected for the sample. This principle can be violated in a number of ways: if, for example, the selection of respondents is influenced by the values of the researcher, or if the list from which a sample is drawn does not completely enumerate the population of interest, or if the list follows some peculiar sequence, or if sections of the population are difficult to contact or refuse to co-operate.

Unless care is taken to minimise biases of this kind, careful calculations of precision will be to no avail; our estimate of the population value will be wrong. It is not enough for researchers to assume that if they do not make conscious decisions when selecting their sample randomness will be assured. This is not so; experience shows that biases can creep in in extremely subtle ways, and that researchers can, quite unconsciously, favour some groups and disfavour others. The only way to ensure randomness is to make sample selections independent of human judgement. There are several techniques for doing this, the most common of which is to select a sample drawn from a list, called a sampling frame, according to the numbers given in a table of random numbers, or by a random number generator. If, on the other hand, the researcher can be sure there is no ordering in the list from which he samples, that the list itself is random in other words, it will be quite in order to adopt a procedure known as systematic sampling from lists, which involves selecting every *n*th name or house as required.

Although the simple random sampling procedures just described allow us to make definite statements about likely accuracy, it is still possible for extremely unlucky events to occur, and for the sample we draw to be unrepresentative of the population in terms of a variable that is believed to be very important for the study being undertaken. To meet this possibility, and so increase precision, a technique known as stratification is employed.[12] Essentially this involves dividing the population into groups or strata and sampling randomly within each. If the differences between strata are maximised and the variations within them minimised, the benefits from the stratification can be considerable. Stratification is a technique which can greatly help a large survey since the sample size can be kept to a small number. The problem with this is that it tends to maximise the geographical dispersion of the sample within the population, so increasing travel and other costs. An alternative procedure to stratification involves concentrating the sample within selected subgroups, or clusters, of the population which makes interviewing more convenient by concentrating respondents together. However, it reduces precision and leaves room for biases. Nevertheless, there are special reasons why clustering may be used, such as when an investigator is interested in certain subgroups of the total population. But, by and large, neither of these procedures recommended themselves to the early survey researchers in this country, such as Bowley. His procedure was to compromise between administrative convenience and representativeness by using more than one stage of sampling. He chose a sample of towns for his study as a first stage, then selected smaller districts within these, and so on. Multi-stage surveys of this kind are most effective if the sampling units are carefully stratified at each stage.[13]

The great achievement, then, of these early surveys was to have provided the techniques for surveying large populations cheaply and within calculable degrees of accuracy. Though the emphasis in social science has shifted from descriptive to analytical surveys and the large-scale national study largely abandoned, except perhaps by the state, the legacies of sampling and survey design remain.

We now turn to the consideration of the early use of social surveys in America. These were scarcely more analytic or explanatory in their approach but were interested in a different kind of data, and developed different techniques for dealing with the problem of representativeness, solved in this country by random sampling.

Early attitude surveys

Primarily, the early social surveys in this country were concerned with discovering the material conditions in which the population lived. They showed little interest in attitudes or opinions. This explains their insistence on 'factual questions', precise and exact, in order to claim that this research yielded 'hard' data.

In the USA different political traditions, among other things, gave rise to a different use of social surveys. This involved the attempt to measure opinion as a guide to action, a quite radical departure. In England, despite the early development of forms of democratic political institutions, public opinion as such had never been a powerful political lever. In contrast to this, over a century ago Abraham Lincoln is reported to have commented on the importance of public opinion in the USA. 'With public opinion on its side, everything succeeds. With public opinion against it, nothing succeeds.'[14]

The conception behind the two early kinds of survey first developed in the United States, the market survey and the pre-election poll, was that whatever people said about their tastes, feelings, beliefs, attitudes, or opinions was a reliable guide to how they would behave. The answers to survey questions could be a guide to behaviour in at least two important ways. First, a survey could be used to predict behaviour, say, of how the electorate would vote or whether people would buy a new product. Second, a survey could be used as a basis for designing new strategies; useful, for example, for a politician in adopting a new policy, or for a sales manager in trying to sell a new product. Surveys such as these could be seen as potentially powerful instruments for the power-holders.

This kind of survey arose in a political culture very different to that in which the 'factual' survey was developed. It was a political culture which, for one thing, emphasised the democratic assumption that the opinion of the general population was not merely of passing interest but an important guide to show how this population would act and react to various political policies. Thus, it recognised the autonomy and the power of the public. By contrast, the British use of surveys involved finding things out about people in order that representations could be made on their behalf by their 'betters'. In addition there was a prevailing view in the United States that it was neither possible nor desirable to attempt to influence social behaviour and organisations very much. However, one need not be overly cynical to realise that having a good idea of what large masses of people are likely to do could give a competitive advantage to politicians and businessmen.

The early American public opinion surveys were probably little influenced by British social survey work. Little in the way of social problem research was conducted in the United States in the first quarter of this century. Market research surveys probably were the first of the opinion type of survey to be used, as early as the first decade of this century. Abrams explains this early use of the market survey in terms of particular economic factors uniquely encountered in the United States.[15] American firms were among the first to confront a national mass market as opposed to a regional one, the whole of the country being a gigantic free trade area for American firms. For businessmen the question of what consumers wanted and how their product could be most effectively marketed was a vital one and could spell the difference between huge or only small profits and even losses. As a consequence large American firms began to conduct their own market surveys until, increasingly, such work became the specialised trade of advertising agencies.

Attempts to survey the political views of electors began rather later, though they did have similar aspirations to those of the market survey. On the whole they were rather less well conducted. Until recently, Harrisburg, Pennsylvania, was notorious only for the earliest perpetration of a 'straw poll'; an attempt to predict the outcome of the 1924 presidential election. Those surveys conducted by newspapers became notorious for their not infrequent and lamentable failures to come even close to accurate prediction of electoral outcomes. The most famous of these débâcles was the *Literary Digest* Poll of 1936. Despite the success of an earlier poll in 1932 and the distribution of over 10 million questionnaires to respondents selected from telephone directories, the poll failed to predict the election of F. D. Roosevelt.[16]

Such mistakes as these did not, however, entirely discredit the polls. Instead, it encouraged the search for better methods culminating in the quota sample and the opinion research agency. Quota sampling is an attempt to approximate random sampling procedures, but in a way that minimises the practical difficulties of selecting and contacting respondents, so offering considerable advantages in terms of cost and convenience.

Contributions of the early attitude surveys: quota sampling

Instead of seeking a random sample from a population in which each member has a known, calculable, and non-zero probability of inclusion, quota sampling proceeds by deliberately selecting a sample which reflects a known composition of the whole population. These days much is known about the social composition of the population thanks largely to the activity of government through the national census. It is thus possible to make sure that any sample we choose has the same distribution of characteristics as the general population. By selecting for a sample a definite 'quota' which reflects the proportion of people in the general population with the same characteristics, we have, *prima facie*, reason to think the sample representative. The criteria most commonly used to establish how many people we should have in a sample are: age, sex, marital status, and social class, although different criteria may be used in investigations as appropriate. These criteria are called 'quota controls' because they are used to limit the number of respondents chosen within the predetermined quotas.[17]

Strictly speaking, of course, this kind of sampling does not allow statistical theory to be used to make generalisations about the whole population since the selection of cases within the quota category is not done strictly according to random sampling procedures. For this reason, it has attracted heavy criticism from statisticians and methodologists. On the other hand, quota sampling, it could be argued, is informed by sociological principles. Most importantly, the quota sampling procedure takes into account the fact that people in different social circumstances will have different views; and the sample is chosen so that more salient features and differences that are thought to exist are proportionately represented. To some extent this aim can be achieved by stratifying a random sample appropriately in the manner discussed in the previous section. But there are very often insurmountable practical difficulties in doing this. It is very difficult, for example, to stratify in advance a sampling list such as an electoral register by social class or education. Random sampling, it might be argued, makes rather few concessions to the fact that human populations are not socially well mixed: indeed, they tend, by and large, to develop a distinct homogeneity within subgroups. Quota sampling, intelligently used, can deal with these difficulties effectively.

Instead of all the difficulties of finding or developing an appropriate sampling frame, and of drawing the sample randomly from the list, the quota sample is usually drawn by the interviewer. The researcher goes out looking for respondents who conform to quota requirements, either by knocking on doors, or, sometimes, by simply asking people in the street to participate. To do this without quota controls would be extremely dangerous. To include all the people in a particular street could be to take people of rather similar income and, therefore, consumption habits. To select respondents in the High Street on a Monday, would be to include an excessive proportion of women of child-bearing age. Quotas go some way to ensuring that the researcher does not introduce such biases. By working the High Street on a Monday, the interviewer will rapidly fill the quota of married women 20–35, and possibly of men and women over 65, but he or she will probably have to look elsewhere for men of other ages and social classes. Researchers using quotas have to ask a number of preliminary questions to ensure that people encountered do fulfil quota requirements, and if they do not, politely break off the interview. There are obvious difficulties with this, of which the main ones are, firstly, that asking personal questions is not always the best way to begin an interview and so may produce a large number of refusals which may itself introduce a bias. Secondly, it is a great temptation for an interviewer to classify respondents into categories where they are most needed rather than where they really belong, especially when the job is nearly complete and respondents from particular categories seem particularly rare.

However, properly used, the quota sample will avoid the grosser errors made by attitude surveys in the past. On this point it seems that the *Literary Digest* Poll and others like it were subject to two forms of bias. First, non-response was high, and it is more than possible that those who did not respond had different views from those who did. Second, the lists actually used for the sample were unrepresentative of the whole population. Owning a telephone, for example, implies a certain minimum of income and life style, and using telephone owners as the sampling list would seriously over-represent the better off and, presumably, more politically conservative sections of the population.

In view of the comparatively greater possibilities of error, it is perhaps surprising that the early polls came so close as they did in predicting election outcomes. After all, the *Literary Digest* Poll for the 1932 election came within a tiny margin of the actual result. This in itself heightened expectations of the accuracy of the prediction for 1936. Looked at against the background of the difficulties in the way of achieving a representative sample discussed earlier in this chapter, the close result of 1932 was a fantastic stroke of luck; and errors of 4 per cent or so, as produced in 1936, are only to be expected. However, by the introduction of a quota sample procedure as briefly described much greater accuracy was achieved in the predictions derived from such research. On the basis of extremely small samples, only a few thousand in each of a number of selected states, it proved possible to make quite accurate estimates of the outcome of American presidential elections. This is itself quite an achievement in view of the size of the electorate in the USA. In 1948, three of the main American polls wrongly predicted the outcome of the election, causing some political controversy. In that election Truman won (taking 49.5 per cent of the votes cast) and Dewey lost (taking 45.1 per cent of the votes). The Gallup Poll predicted 49.5 per cent for Dewey and 44.5 per cent for Truman. Although as a prediction of the election result the sample figures were misleading, neither estimate (for the votes cast for Dewey and Truman) is more than a few per cent out. For purposes other than election forecasting such close estimates would be extremely useful, if carefully used.

Since the interwar period, when quota sampling was first developed in the USA, it has been refined to a high art by commercial research organisations in many countries of the Western world.

The chief merits of quota sampling are its cheapness and administrative convenience. Such samples can be interviewed very quickly at a tiny fraction of the cost of a full-scale national random sample. Thus, for certain purposes, such as market surveys and pre-election polls, they are probably not to be improved upon. In recent years there have been a number of attempts to develop random sampling procedures as quick and as cheap as quotas. The Marplan survey is a contemporary British example. However, there is little evidence to show that samples drawn on a random basis give estimates of opinions which are more accurate for these purposes than those yielded by carefully selected quota samples. Indeed, for some purposes its cheapness and speed may make quota sampling a procedure which could be used more extensively in some academic research, where a general indication of the attitudes extant in a specified population is required. Moreover, it is possible to incorporate elements of randomness into quota sampling by rejecting numbers of possible respondents according to a random sequence.

So far in this chapter we have described two uses of the survey method which developed initially outside of academic institutions. Through the eyes of contemporary methodologists the instrumental assumptions informing these might seem naïve. They took, for example, a relatively unsophisticated view of the elements we considered at the end of Chapter 2: behaviour, ideas, and speech. For the early British surveyors, surveys were a means of obtaining from large numbers of people reports on their conditions of life, while the early American attitude surveyors were more interested in the attitudes and opinions which would predispose people to behave in accordance with those attitudes or opinions. Today, however, both of these uses of the survey have been superseded, at least in academic circles; a development made possible by developments in social and statistical theory.

In this it was scholars in the United States who took the lead. Social science and social research had become an established and thriving part of the academic community from the beginning of this century. By contrast, social science in this country was starved of funds and personnel; having no foothold in the élite establishments of further education, it made little progress. In those institutions where the social sciences, especially sociology, were taught, principally the London School of Economics, they seemed to concentrate more on developing a theoretical tradition than a social research one. The theoretical tradition they did sustain was that of social liberalism developing the evolutionary and organicist elements of this approach into elaborate bodies of theoretical ideas. As a result, there is an unbroken strand of social liberal philosophy in British social thought from L. T. Hobhouse, Professor of Sociology at LSE from 1903 to 1929, through Morris Ginsberg, 1929–54, and down to T. H. Marshall in the postwar period.[18] The outlook of these men, particularly Ginsberg and Hobhouse, was evolutionary and comparative, scarcely connecting with the strictly factual investigations of Bowley, Boyd Orr, and Caradog-Jones. In this country only social anthropology among the social sciences achieved significant theoretical development based on empirical research and attracted widespread institutional support.

The contrast with what occurred in the USA could hardly be

more sharp. In that country, three great universities, Chicago, Columbia, and Harvard pioneered the development of sociology. Sociology was institutionalised throughout the university sector in America before the Second World War.[19] J. D. Y. Peel, reviewing the development of the social sciences suggests that 'sociology was made a reasonably unified subject by the Americans who welded together very diverse streams', which, by the 1940s, 'was being synthesised into a mainstream of theory to which most ongoing research was related'.[20] It is certainly true that the most active social science departments gave rise successively to: the approach to social science which developed participant observation, the use of the survey method as a means to the examination of attitudes and personality, and, last but not least, the modern sociological use of the survey to corroborate theoretical accounts of social organisation. Our concern here is with the latter part of these developments. But before any of them could take place several years of theoretical exploration and search had to take place.

In the United States, as in Britain and Europe, there has been a recurrent and problematic divide between theory and research data. In the one, broad speculation seemed to need little in the way of systematic data collection, while in the empirical study of social life, broad theories seemed to be of little relevance. It is possible to produce a sizeable list of American sociologists, all eminent scholars, who seldom undertook on their own account, systematic data collection of the kind considered either in this chapter or in Chapter 4, but relied in the main on their own convictions or on secondary sources of various kinds. Such a list would have to include W. G. Summer, R. M. MacIver, A. Small, P. A. Sorokin, C. H. Cooley, and R. E. Park. For our purposes it is important to note the character of their involvement with data. They were eclectic in the kind of data they sought and rather unsystematic in the use they made of it.

Martindale charts the intellectual history of American sociology from the interwar period to post Second World War as a movement from the dominance of social behaviourism to that of functionalism. He suggests, too, that shifts in the social and political climate in the United States may have had something to do with this change. He writes:

...the very dates of the steep rise of interest in functionalism among sociological theorists also suggests that it may have some ideological import. It rose after 1940, and with particular speed after the Second World War. Moreover, its ranks have been increasingly swelled by deserters from social behaviorism – an evidently liberal position. The rise of sociological functionalism thus coincides with the return of the Republican Party to power, the return to religion, the rise of McCarthyism, and other typical manifestations of a postwar conservative reaction.[21]

Whether postwar social science is really more conservative than what preceded it is difficult to say. But, as we have already emphasised, the character of social science will be strongly influenced by its social, political, and economic context. There are additional factors important in this case. In Chapter 1 we remarked that intellectual disciplines are developed by social groups; and, in the United States during the period we are discussing, there were powerful moves for the professionalisation of sociology and social science. The main manifestations of this were the insistence on education to the doctorate level for recruits to the discipline, and the development of theoretical and methodological orthodoxies in teaching and research. The orthodoxies which came to be established were functionalist theory and, in methods, the survey.[22]

Prior to the culmination of these developments we have just noted, the various branches of social behaviourism were well represented in the major American universities. As is to be expected, there were major differences of viewpoint both within and between these institutions. Indeed, only by holding to a very diffuse understanding of social theory is it possible to see these views and their exponents as representatives of the same general theoretical approach. This theoretical diffuseness and disagreement was paralleled by a marked degree of confusion over the appropriate research methods to use in empirical studies. An eclectic use of data was the order of the day. At this time little contribution was made to the technique of social survey. Symbolic interactionism was perhaps the most vigorous of the variants of social behaviourism, having a firm foundation in the University of Chicago.[23] Here, as we shall see in Chapter 5, participant observation rather than the survey was held to be the most fruitful method of social research.

Perhaps one can gauge the general attitude to data from seminal pieces of empirical research from the period in question. A frequently cited example from the early years of Chicago is the study by Thomas and Znanieki, *The Polish Peasant in Europe and America*.[24] The bulk of the data used for this study were documentary: letters from Polish peasants to relatives living in America, the archives of Polish newspapers, and the records and periodicals of Polish *émigré* organisations. Also included was the autobiography of a young Pole, running to some 300 pages. This material is subjected to analysis, and forms the basis of an account of the social changes in rural Poland, the attempts on the part of emigrating peasants to retain elements of their cultural identity, and their eventual imperfect integration into American society. But there is no attempt at the systematic analysis of these documents by statistical treatment of either their numbers or content. There is also no attempt to supplement documentary material with systematic interviews, though from the text it is clear that both authors talked to many Poles in the course of their investigation. However, the point to notice is how the kind of data deemed ideal for the investigation has been defined: intimate life-histories, including accounts of motivation and interaction, are seen as being central. How best to elicit these is not, however, so clear. Thomas and Znanieki seem to have collected only very few life histories of their subjects.

An equally celebrated empirical study was that undertaken by Robert and Helen Lynd working from Columbia in 1924–25. This was a study of life in Muncie, Indiana.[25] Here there is even greater eclecticism in the sources of data. Not only did these investigators undertake extensive analysis of any documents they could find, but they used a whole range of other data collection practices as well. These included the compilation and consideration of official and other statistics from municipal and state records; the participation of members of the research team in community events and institutions; depth interviews with large numbers of people; and, finally, a standardised questionnaire was administered to various sets of individuals. Although the survey using questionnaires does make an appearance in this study, it is merely an additional method of data collection among a number of others. It is by no means the most important of the methods used; participation in social life and the consideration of documentary material is given far more prominence than any sort of interviewing or survey work.

However, between the mid-1920s and the mid-1960s in America there is a marked and dramatic shift towards the dominance of survey methods in social research. A study of the kind of research published in the official journal of the American Sociological Association for the years 1962 to 1969, showed that 90 per cent of the articles and research notes presented data taken from social surveys using questionnaires. A small number of studies were based on participation, but a high proportion of these also included supplementary interview data 'to bolster their conclusions'. Brown and Gilmartin also report that, 'Other anthropological techniques were completely ignored. Life histories and personal documents were seldom gathered.'[26]

Associated with this rise to prominence of the survey are new modes of theorising about social action and social organisation. As a result a different kind of social survey emerged and with it new kinds of data. In the next sections we will consider these.

The social psychological survey

During the 1930s the interest in public opinion polling germinated a more academic interest in attitudes. In part this was an attempt, as we shall see, to solve some of the problems arising from election prediction. At this time and throughout the 1940s and 1950s a series of attempts were made to take the problems of attitude measurement, and the related issue of the relationship between attitudes and behaviour, very seriously indeed. One of the more immediate problems to which this effort was directed was the prediction of election results, partly no doubt because of its topicality, partly because this problem could attract research funds.

In America, what we now recognise as social psychology has always been a rich vein of thought. Not only have Americans made seminal contributions to the origins of this discipline, but many American sociologists have been imbued with an interest in small-group phenomena, and the extent to which social learning is influenced by imitation or instinct. Scholars such as Giddings, Thomas, and Znanieki are often considered as contributors to the basic ideas of social psychology as well as to sociology.[27] Scholars in this field had for some time been engaged in a debate over the relative importance of acquired and inherent personality traits in behaviour. Attitude research was the property of no school in this respect, and though it by no means resolved the issue itself, it did constitute an area of debate to which all might contribute.

At this time, too, the vigorous indigenous current of thought and research in social psychology in America was given a powerful boost by an influx of expatriate German scholars, liberal democrats most of them, who were fleeing from Hitler's regime. Kurt Lewin, Jacob L. Moreno, and Theodore Adorno are perhaps the best known of these. The work of these men, which was primarily experimental, was not in the main concerned with social surveys. It contributed to American social psychology by suggesting new theories of personality and personality formation inspired by a very different European tradition of thought.

Also, in the 1930s and 1940s such men as Lazarsfeld, Thurstone, Stouffer and Guttman, had begun to develop a quite different approach to attitudes than had previously been considered. Instead of taking attitudes as relatively straightforward guides to behaviour, they sought to measure attitudes as properties of human thought. They reasoned that an attitude held by an individual is a unique value on a continuum of possibilities, rather than something which is either present or absent. Hence, instead of asking a voter whether or not he intends to vote Republican, they would ask a battery of questions bearing on many aspects of Republican policies. This was, in itself, not a radical departure from opinion poll methods, and Gallup and other agencies were soon to develop similar techniques. But the procedures used here were more than simple attempts to improve the sensitivity of attitude measures. They also involved no little theoretical reformulation. Ultimately, it was assumed that what was being measured was a property of the human mind. How that property came to be, and what its ultimate characteristics might be, were issues which rapidly came on to the agenda of these researchers, and are matters which are even now imperfectly resolved. Yet, as an attempt to explain human behaviour this approach is a genuine innovation for social science. From verbal responses, the researcher infers a model of the interviewee's personality, and it is by reference to this, rather than the attitude itself, that behaviour is explained. This is a procedure which is common to a large number of scaling exercises in social research today.

The study which pushed the techniques discussed here furthest in the direction of theorising about personality on the basis of attitude survey data is the celebrated work of T. W. Adorno and others reported in *The Authoritarian Personality*.[28] In this study several discrete attitude scales were used: the so-called Anti-Semitism, Ethnocentricity, Political Conservatism and Fascism scales. The scales themselves were devised in a manner originally invented by American social psychologist Rensis Lickert.[29] The questionnaire used for the survey began with a few brief factual questions about personal details; while a second more important part of the schedule contained batteries of questions aimed at measuring an individual's standing on the scales mentioned above. For the authors of this study there was a clear expectation that individuals would commonly produce patterned responses on their scales, which could be ascribed to a certain type of personality. In particular the kind they were most interested in was exemplified by individuals scoring highly on each of their scores which they called the 'Authoritarian Personality'. Such personalities were seen by these writers as objectifying within the personality a particular sort of social and political ideology, which was also the product of determinable social processes.

Chief legacies of social psychological surveys

These developments in social psychology have made available a whole series of highly sophisticated techniques for measuring attitudes. Though these techniques are not used so extensively, or exclusively, as they once were in America, and they have never been extensively used in Britain, the achievements of these writers have inevitably influenced the work of modern survey analysts in the way that they compose survey questions and analyse the results.

But it was not only the structure of attitudes that concerned these scholars but also their dynamics. Attitudes can be changed in response to many kinds of stimuli, election campaigns, advertising, social interaction, and so on, sometimes in ways crucial for understanding or predicting the outcome of events. Elections, for example, are not decided by those electors whose support for particular parties is relatively fixed, but by those relatively uncommitted individuals whose attitudes and voting choice may not become set until polling day. Presumably on many issues, and in many situations, attitudes in everyday life do change and may change rapidly. Recognising this problem led this group of writers to make the first serious use of what are called longitudinal studies.[30]

The surveys we have discussed so far in this chapter have all involved taking a single cross-section sample of a particular population, on the assumption that the results of the survey would give reliable information about the whole. If, however, we take cognisance of the possibility of change then, clearly, such a procedure has its pitfalls. For one, if we administer as part of a cross-section survey a series of attitude questions to a sample of respondents we will be unlikely to determine which of those respondents are expressing attitudes which are fairly firm and durable, and those who are merely responding out of some whim or other, maybe to please the interviewer or to get rid of him quickly. Moreover, in a particularly volatile period, such as the run-up to an election, all kinds of events may predispose some people to change their attitudes, and it may well be important to chart this movement in order to decide if it is systemic or spasmodic. In an effort to meet these and other problems Lazarsfeld and colleagues devised the 'panel study'. With this procedure they recruited a sample of people to a panel, and surveyed their attitudes at different times. This method had the merit of allowing researchers to identify changes in attitudes among a population in a way that was more reliable than repeated random sampling, where variations might simply be due to variations between different samples. Provided that the panel was selected on a random basis in the first place, we can be sure that the changes that are identified are real changes in the group and, within a given limit of reliability, in the population as well.

Sometimes control samples are selected as well to check on the effects of repeated interviewing.[31]

Panel studies are an example of longitudinal studies which are, of course, not confined to attitude research. In the form of 'cohort studies', that is, following single age groups through successive periods, they have proved extremely useful in medical, environmental, and policy-related research. Unfortunately, such survey designs are also costly which is perhaps the major reason why they tend to be little used.

We can now turn to our final type of survey.

The explanatory social survey

First of all it is necessary to say a word about the name given to the type of survey we are about to discuss. In a way, all the survey types we have considered so far have been concerned with explanation, at least in a wide sense of this term. What we have in mind here are uses of the survey which are designed to test particular explanations or theories. As such it involves using the survey as a structure which, through its very design, allows for the testing of hypotheses derived systematically from a theory. This procedure was consequent on developments in statistical methodology, as we shall see.

Just as an earlier generation of social survey researchers in Britain had made use of developments in statistics to promote their activities, so did the postwar generation of social scientists in the United States. The eventual outcome of these developments was, as we noted before, the emergence of the social survey as the dominant method of research using design principles adapted from biology and botany.

For many years biologists and botanists had been concerned with developing methods of eliminating extraneous variables in their research, so that the effect of the factor in which they were primarily interested could be more effectively gauged. For example, in evaluating the yield of a particular hybrid plant, they had to be certain that all the factors which, collectively, affect growth, such as climate, fertility of the soil, moisture, disease resistance, and so on, were adequately controlled so that the yield of the hybrid could be stringently compared with the yield of the non-hybrid. In this way observed differences in yields, or whatever property was being investigated, could be isolated as due to genetic or to the various environmental factors. The techniques which emerged to deal with this kind of problem owed much to the pioneering work of R. A. Fisher and others, and involved elaboration on the classic form of experimental design.[32]

In this design a control group is used to assess the relationship between some causal factor and its presumed effect. In trying to determine the effect of a causal factor, for example, the effect of teaching style on academic attainment, factors extraneous to this relationship but which might affect, in this example, academic attainment, need to be excluded, so that the relationship of interest can be examined and its effects accurately assessed. One common strategy of achieving this is to use a control group matched member for member with the experimental group. The presumed causal factor, normally called the 'independent variable', is withheld from the control group. Accordingly, since the two groups are alike in all respects except that one of them, namely the experimental group, has received the causal 'treatment', then any differences in, to use our example, academic attainment, must be due to chance or the additional factor. There are a whole set of statistical techniques for measuring the probability that the observed differences between the two groups could have resulted from chance. Such tests yield statements of probability about the likelihood of a particular result having occurred by chance. This is what is meant when it is reported that a result, according to a particular test, is significant at, say, the 0.01 level. That is, it would be probability of 1 in 100 for this result to have happened by chance. Because this is a low probability, the researcher could feel justified in accepting the result of the experiment as, at least, very probably demonstrating a causal connection.

Of course, the major problem is ensuring that the experimental and the control groups are as alike as possible in all relevant respects. Accordingly, the researcher needs to know a great deal about likely extraneous factors so that he can control them. In the example here it might be concluded that the age of the pupils may well influence attainment or otherwise modify the effects of the causal factor. It would, therefore, be verging on the absurd to have one group composed of 8-year-olds and the other of 16-year-olds. In this case the researcher has the choice of restricting his sample to one age group, or increasing the sample size to include all age ranges.

When the researcher is satisfied that his group contains the subjects with the characteristics he wants, the job then is to allocate them to, respectively, the experimental and the control group. Of course, there may be other factors of which the investigator is unaware. Also, it may be that some surreptitious influence will affect his choice of which subjects to allocate to the groups. Therefore, the subjects need to be paired so that each pair consists of subjects matched on all relevant characteristics, and the allocation of a member of the pair to a group made randomly. Matching and random allocation are the two key principles here.[33]

It is this logical model which, as a research design, has been used to considerable effect in some branches of psychology and medicine as a way of testing causal explanations. It is also a model adopted by contemporary survey research, though in a much truncated form. The degree of control of human populations required by the random allocation of individuals to experimental or control groups, and subjecting one but not the other to the experimental treatment is, under field conditions, practically impossible. This is not to mention the possible moral objections that might arise. Only approximations to the full requirements of the model can be met. In place of the random allocation to different groups, survey analysts have to be content with random samples from different groups which occur naturally in the population. In place of the controlled administration of a 'treatment', survey analysts have to ensure that individuals with different experiences or attitudes are represented in the samples by stratification, or a similar procedure. Neither practice has anything like the rigour of the procedures required by the model. In fact, much of the use of experimental design in survey work takes place at the data analysis stage through elaborations of the cross-tabulation technique, as we shall see later in this chapter.[34]

Although this use of the survey seemed to offer to social sciences a more scientific way of approximating more closely to a natural scientific model of research, it has not been without its controversies. One such concerned the validity of statistical testing upon which much of the analysis seemed to depend. During the 1950s one group of American scholars vigorously attacked the use of statistical tests, pointing out the difficulty of meeting the logical requirements demanded by the statistical theory, especially that of random allocation.[35] Unless this condition was met the tests were simply inappropriate: they could tell us nothing. The defence against this attack largely took the form of admitting that such tests could not be used to infer proof, since the condition pointed out earlier could not be met, but, none the less, were valuable indicators of possibly significant or interesting relationships in the data. What both groups of protagonists did agree on was that the use of statistical tests without a well-thought-out theory was little more than useless. In other words, statistical testing should not be used as a substitute for ideas by searching the data for any significant relationships that happen to be there. In other words, they agree that it is the theoretical significance of a relationship found in the data that is much more important than the statistical significance.

Raising the issue of theory is extremely important in connection with this type of survey, and it is time to attempt some evaluation of the method. As we have already said, the aim of this type of survey, unlike the other types we have looked at, is to test sociological theories by modelling the design of the survey itself on some principles from the logic of experiments. Moreover, use is also made of statistical tests, largely derived from work originally done in botany and biology, to measure the significance of relationships found in the data as additional evidence for or against the hypothesis being tested. Unfortunately, it has to be admitted that in a number of respects this use of the survey fails to match up to the very strict requirements predicated by the logic of experiments. Let us examine one or two of these issues in more detail.

The normal practice of surveyors in this tradition is to select their groups of interest and randomly sample within these, normally from an appropriate list, such as an electoral register, employment record, or whatever is at hand and best fits the requirements of full coverage of the population to be sampled. The survey is then carried out, the data collected and processed. The logic of the experiment is used at the next stage, namely, during the analysis of the data collected. Unfortunately, in an important sense this is too late a stage. As we said at the beginning, the classical experimental design requires two groups, a control and an experimental group, to which subjects are allocated according to the principles of matching and randomisation. In this way, prior to the experimental treatment, the two groups are as alike, in all respects, as they can be. However, in field conditions, nothing like this is ever attempted, for obvious practical reasons. What happens is that the data analyst groups the subjects into what are homogeneous categories according to some relevant characteristic or variable. Thus, he might construct categories according to type of occupation, say, manual or non-manual. Now, obviously, although the respondents so grouped will all have this characteristic in common respectively, they will undoubtedly vary on lots of other factors, such as level of education, hair colour, type of housing, income, tastes in music, number of children, etc. Some of the more salient of these the analyst may try to control by, for example, dividing each of his two original groups into those who are married and those who are unmarried. In this way, so the argument goes, the effect of occupational type can be explored on some variable, say, political affiliation, holding marital status constant.

But let us notice one or two points about this procedure. First, a practical point but none the less important for all that, there is a limit to the number of variables which can be held constant in this way. After two or three the researchers would soon run out of cases. The original sample would have to be huge to enable him, or her, to go much beyond this. Second, and not unrelated to the first, the hypothesis being tested cannot be properly tested since all possible confounding factors have not been controlled or randomised. In the classic experimental design all other confounding factors are designed out to highlight the one which the researcher is interested in examining. In natural situations it may well be that many of the so-called confounding factors do interact with the causal relationship being tested, but that is not the point as far as the experiment is concerned. By matching and randomisation they are controlled out so that the researcher can examine a relationship between a cause and its effect in its pure, uncluttered form. It is too late to achieve even an approximation to this at this stage of data analysis. An example of these difficulties is to be found in a study by Powers into the causes of delinquency. This study is one of the few attempts to use full experimental designs in field-work conditions. He carefully matched his subjects and randomly allocated them to control and experimental groups to test the effect of 'warm and friendly counsel' on the prevention of delinquency. Unfortunately, 'warm and friendly counsel' lacked the precision required for the definition of an independent variable in experimental testing, since the counsellor's conception of what this constituted varied considerably. Accordingly, these variant practices collectively called 'warm and friendly counsel' constituted uncontrolled factors that the design did not recognise.[36] Third, a survey can only ask people about a limited range of things and, as a consequence, the data analyst can only control those factors on which he has data. This is true of the experiment but, by the process of random allocation of matched individuals to groups, these other factors of which the experimenter is unaware are randomised in their effects. A survey researcher cannot assume this at all. Look at the two groups used for illustration here: manual and non-manual workers. Though a conscientious researcher might endeavour to ask questions about all the kinds of things that could possibly have a bearing on political affiliation there are limits. But can he be confident that he has covered everything? The answer is no. But are these other possible factors randomised? This is rather harder to answer, and raises an issue of some fundamental importance.

In the example we are using here – and it is not too far away from survey practice – the researcher has selected his sample according to some random selection procedure. Only later are the groups divided with respect to the property of occupational type. However, this is hardly the randomisation required by the logic of experimental design. In this case randomisation is designed to dispel the effects of factors which might confound the relationship of interest, while in the case of the survey this is not so. It might be a reasonable approximation to experimental randomisation if it can be assumed that the population from which the sample is drawn is homogeneous; a reasonable assumption to make when one is dealing with a population of seeds, plants, germs, or other simpler organisms. It is not a reasonable assumption, we would suggest, when dealing with human populations. Indeed, one might add here, that the very idea of a control group was devised to cope with the peculiarities of human subjects as opposed to non-human ones, especially effects produced by the use of research itself.[37] But, in any event, one of the fundamental assumptions of sociology, indeed of social science as a whole, is that individuals are related to each other in complex ways. They are members of groups, cultures, and subcultures, live in communities, in families, are mobile, and so forth; dimensions which are virtually ignored when individuals are sampled in the way indicated here. Further, comparing categories or groups, such as manual or non-manual workers, of socially unrelated individuals can be no substitute for examining the group life in which individuals actually live and interact.

However, one could argue that this need not matter if the researcher is interested in testing hypotheses about individuals and not about groups. Nevertheless, the effects of these group influences would still have to be controlled in some way and controlled during the selection process. Attempting to control during the stage of data analysis is not possible for the reasons we have already set out.

There is another way in which this kind of criticism may be met. It can be argued that although the surveyor might sample individuals, these can be asked to report on any affiliations which the researcher feels important to his main hypothesis. After all, this is claimed to be one of the main strengths of the survey: that is, obtaining information through interviews about a whole host of topics. In other words, by using the medium of speech the interviewer can gather data from respondents on their thoughts, deeds, aspirations, beliefs, etc. There are, as we might expect, problems about this which we shall deal with in Chapter 4.

Conclusion

In this chapter we have concentrated on matters to do with the design of four types of surveys. The types themselves arise from the varying purposes each was constructed to serve. The first, what we called the 'factual survey', originated in efforts to produce 'facts' about the material conditions in which the population of the country lived. In this sense the survey aimed at achieving an economical description of the material state of society at a particular point in time. In a similar fashion the 'attitude survey' aimed at the same goal but concentrated on rather different data, namely, attitudes and opinions. Both faced the problem of using a part, a sample, from which to generalise about the whole, the society itself. To this end sampling techniques were borrowed and developed to effect such inferences. With one or two exceptions, these kinds of surveys have dropped out of academic usage but remain important data collection methods for government agencies, market researchers, and opinion pollsters.

The third and fourth types of survey we identified begin to move towards explicitly using surveys to provide data relevant to the testing or exploration of social scientific theories. The 'social psychological surveys', for example, were instrumental in developing a body of knowledge dealing with the relationship of attitudes and personality to social behaviour. In doing so, they raised methodological problems of some significance; including the relationship of attitudes to behaviour, the relationship between what respondents say and what they think and do, the problem of attitude change and identifying real change from spurious change, and so on. Some of these had ramifications for the other types of survey we have discussed, and efforts at solution of them created a set of techniques, such as the attitude scale, and the panel study, still used in social research.

The last type of survey discussed, the 'explanatory survey', represents a research tool devised to test hypotheses about social behaviour, using a logic derived from experiments and incorporating powerful statistical tests. It is a design felt by many to indicate the coming of the social sciences to scientific maturity: a rigorous method to explore causal relationships among social phenomena and, ultimately, discover the laws of social life. Unfortunately, as we have suggested, matters are not so straightforward. For one thing, the design of such surveys contravene many of the required assumptions of experimental design and, as a consequence, vitiate the use of statistical tests which crucially depend on those assumptions. In making this criticism we drew attention to the matter of sampling and raised points which we can bring to bear on all the survey types we have discussed.

The earlier use of sampling theory was aimed at providing a basis for the estimation of population values from a subset or sample of the larger population. In other words, representativeness was the crucial criterion of an adequate sample. Important, too, in drawing a sample of this kind, is some precise delimitation of the population. Sampling requires a listing of the population members, whatever they may be, from which the sample may be drawn according to a random procedure. Accordingly, if one wishes to produce a sample to estimate the prevalence of certain characteristics in the population of the United Kingdom, one has to be able, in principle, to list that population. In a case like this, however, substitutes to this ideal are normally used, such as electoral registers, list of households, etc. with the proviso that such lists, while convenient, may not include, for any number of reasons, all we would wish to define as belonging to the population of the United Kingdom. Providing that such lists do not seriously under-represent significant subgroups, reasonably good samples can be drawn using them for this purpose.

Unfortunately, such a procedure is not always suitable for hypothesis-testing research since here the aim is to achieve sufficient cases for analysis rather than a sample representative of the larger whole. In some respects it is perhaps less appropriate to speak of samples at all in the case of explanatory surveys. What is necessary here, to repeat, are cases which possess relevant characteristics; that is, those of interest to the surveyor. Thus, sampling, or the selection of cases, needs to be done on the basis of theoretically informed criteria rather than by reference to some ideal of representativeness. To see what this might involve let us look at a rather more serious and fundamental issue relevant to both the descriptive and the explanatory uses of the survey.

The survey makes use of the interview and/or the question-naire: a method of data collection obviously designed to be given to individuals. As a result the sampling units are ultimately, even if stratification or other similar devices are used, individuals. It is the responses they provide which constitute the data which are recorded and analysed. Moreover, it is individuals, in one capacity or another, who appear on lists which can, for the good reason of convenience, be used by the surveyor to select a sample. However, here we come across a possible disjunction, and one we have hinted at earlier, between the instrumental pre-suppositions of the survey and the more theoretical conceptions of social science. It is a banal but crucial postulate underpinning all the social sciences that individuals are related through associ-ations and groups of various kinds. They are located within many networks of roles and relationships, neighbourhood, work, fam-ily, an economic system, a polity, they are stratified according to various criteria, have differential life chances bequeathed by birth and attainment, and so forth: in short, it is not so much the isolated individual, or even a large number of isolated indi-viduals, that is the focus of interest, but individuals-in-relation-to-other-individuals. In this respect, then, it can be argued that the survey is too individualistic, not only in the sense that only individuals can respond to questionnaires but also in that a proba-bility model is involved in the sampling procedure so that the individual is removed from his, or her, social context and, as Galtung puts it, 'made to appear in the sample as a society of one person to be compared with other societies of one person'.[38] The only way in which such a procedure might be excused is if the societies from which the samples were drawn were homogene-ous: an assumption, one would argue, dangerous to make with respect to *any* society. Although individuals may be grouped together on the basis of their scores on various variables, such as attitudes, beliefs, etc. this is often without effective regard for their position within the social structure. As a result the social process is lost. The extent to which individuals may suddenly act together, the ways in which new groups may form, or old ones die, are all lost sight of. Instead, predictions are made on the basis of X per cent of a sample having Y attitude quite with-out regard to the differential position of these, and other, individuals in the social structure and the fact that attitudes, etc. may change or be reinforced by changing group allegiances.

There are, as we mentioned earlier in this chapter, ways which claim to deal with this excessive individualism. For one, the sampling procedure could be revised so that individuals are selected according to their structural position rather than according to some random sampling procedure. Such purposive sampling could, for example, sample individuals along with other individuals with whom they are significantly related, such as members of their family, stated friends, work-mates, or whatever is appropriate. A second method is to collect information on structural and other contextual properties, and emphasise this in the analysis rather than the expressed attitude. Clearly, this will have to go further than the usual 'background questions' on occupation, age, education, and so on, normally included in every questionnaire. Details of personal ties and connections and the frequency of such interactions within the individual's life space would have to be sought.

In any event, both of these proposals make surveying much more complicated and difficult to execute. Purposive sampling, for example, could not be effectively done in advance of interview, since 'significant others' could only be guessed at without the information provided by the original informant. Moreover, no attempt could be made to generalise the findings for some predefined population though, in view of what we have said in this chapter, this may be no great loss. As far as incorporating more structural questions in the interview is concerned, this comes against the problem we shall discuss in more detail in the interview chapter; namely, the relationship between what the individual says and what he does.

Galtung suggests that the individualistic survey method may well yield results that reflect the conditions prevailing in one type of society only, that is, societies which rate highly both on individual mobility, geographic, horizontal as well as vertical mobility, and on inner-directedness.[39] Thus, the traditional survey based on random samples from universes of individuals and the effort to account for what they do in terms of an interaction between attitudes, personality and general background structural factors, implies that even if individuals move we can still predict what they do, providing, of course, that we have an adequate theory to cover the relative importance of social position, personality, and the relationship between the two. In other words, we do not require details of significant others since individuals are so inner-directed.

He goes on to make the additional point that social science needs a much richer conception of what constitutes the social unit, bearing in mind that these may well need to change from society to society. The counterpart to the survey in real life is the election. The democratic principle is one person one vote, as in the principle of statistical analysis. Thus, a democratic bias is introduced which may be completely inappropriate where individuals do not count equally, which is in almost all known societies.

It is now time to turn to the interview as a method of data collection nearly always used in conjunction with the survey. Some of the problems we have discussed here will emerge again, and, certainly, the survey should always be evaluated, as a method, in connection with the interview.

4

INTERVIEWING

Interviews in social research are encounters between a researcher and a respondent in which the latter is asked a series of questions relevant to the subject of the research. The respondent's answers constitute the raw data analysed at a later point in time by the researcher. Usually, a questionnaire, sometimes called an interview schedule, is used in the interview and contains the questions the interviewer puts to the respondent. Questionnaires are sometimes used without an interviewer; the respondent completing the questionnaire without any assistance other than the guidance provided through the written instructions on the questionnaire itself. But, in each case they depend on the use of some verbal stimuli – normally a question, but sometimes a statement expressing a point of view – designed to elicit a verbal response which is recorded and, as stated earlier, subsequently analysed as data.

Interviews are normally, though not exclusively, used within a survey research design of some kind. Respondents are selected according to some sampling principle – usually the random or quota procedures discussed in Chapter 3 – designed to select individuals the researcher considers will be representative of some group, property, or process. For example, a researcher interested in the factors responsible for differing rates of absence from work may well interview groups of workers randomly selected from lists of employees in large factories and small ones, factories which have high or low overall rates of absence, or factories which involve different kinds of production process. Any one, or a combination of these, may be chosen as the basis for choosing the workplaces from which a sample can be selected.

Similarly, a researcher interested in the determinants of voting choice might select respondents to interview from an electoral register. Interviewing is not, however, the exclusive preserve of survey research. It is not unusual, for example, to find participant observers using interviews, along with other methods, to collect data. In such cases the interview is used to collect illustrative material to complement other findings. In such cases the issue of representativeness is of less concern than in the sample survey. Yet it must be said that interviewing, especially the formal and standardised type in which questionnaires are used, is much more common in survey research. Effectively, this means standardised interviews using questionnaires are the most common research technique in use at this time.

As we suggested at the beginning of Chapter 3, there must be few people, in industrial societies at least, who have not taken part in an interview as part of a social survey, whether this be for the purposes of public opinion polling or academic research. Of all the methods of data collection available to the contemporary social researcher, the interview, in conjunction with the sample survey, is most typically associated with social research itself. One might well suspect that the choice of the interview method is for many researchers these days more akin to a conditioned reflex than a principled decision. By far the greatest number of reports of academic research published in the field of sociology make use of the interview as a major means of data collection.[1] There are, of course, some obvious practical advantages in the use of interviews and surveys: they represent an economical way of obtaining data in some way relating to the behaviour of large and sometimes scattered populations. But it must be pointed out that there has been a good deal of analysis of the interview method, and particularly of those which involve the use of standardised questions and questionnaires. Although for practical and theoretical reasons the survey involving questionnaire interviews continues to be used, there is a good deal more appreciation of the limitations of this kind of research than hitherto.

Some of the important reasons for this follow from the issues discussed in Chapter 3. As we have seen, although the survey and hence the interviewing practices associated with it have been put to a number of different uses, none of them is without problems. The early surveys, as we have argued, sought facts about people. They, therefore, asked for straightforward factual information, and so specialised in questions which, to quote Bowley, 'require an answer of "yes" or "no" or a simple number or something equally definite and precise'.[2] Though, obviously, contemporary surveys usually involve similar factual questions, such as asking the respondent to give his age or marital status, this sort of information is no longer given the importance it once was. Similarly, the social psychological survey has left a legacy. Contemporary social surveys, as we shall see, usually include attitude questions or items, the form of which has been strongly influenced by the work of those scholars who pioneered the early work we reviewed briefly in Chapter 3. But here again, few would accept that the rationale offered by scholars for the work they did is adequate today. Few contemporary social scientists would suggest that the main aim of their work is simply to measure attitudes accurately, whether or not as part of an attempt to theorise about personality. Finally, as we have also suggested in Chapter 3, it is in the end difficult to sustain a defence of the social survey on the ground that it offers a good approximation to the experimental methods in use in botany, biology, and medicine. Although, clearly, it may be important to consider possible causal connections between the variables measured by the questions asked in a survey, it is rather implausible to suggest that surveys can establish universal or indubitable causal relationships. In sum, though many of the instrumental and theoretical ideas which have underpinned the use of the survey and the interview in the past have been called into question, there is as yet relatively little to replace them.

On the positive side, a good deal of valuable work has been carried out with the interview itself as the focus of research. This among other things, treats the interview as a social event, suggesting that it has social characteristics which may or may not facilitate the collection of data. In the past, the interview tended to be regarded simply as an instrument of no account in itself. Today, social scientists are more aware that many of the instrumental assumptions which are involved in the use of the interview have not been thought about enough from a sociological point of view. This realisation parallels a similar recognition about the need to apply social scientific ideas to the social survey, which was mentioned in Chapter 3. These studies seem to be the most valuable contribution to the development of our knowledge of methods of data collection produced in recent years.

The form the present chapter will take is, therefore, as follows. In the early stages three points will be discussed. Firstly, the sort of rationale offered for the use of the interview in contemporary social research will be reviewed. Secondly, we shall consider both the types of interview that there are and the way in which they commonly feature in social research. Thirdly, we shall address the problems associated with asking questions and constructing questionnaires. Consideration of these matters is very much a ground-clearing exercise. Although this part of our discussion will hopefully be of practical value for those wanting to conduct interviews as part of a research project, there are some more basic issues about the nature and validity of interviews which we regard as most important and which we shall discuss towards the end of the chapter. In later stages of this chapter, then, we suggest that the social research interview is best considered not simply as a technique or as an instrument but as a social process. Obviously, instrumental assumptions will remain an important part of the interview, but our suggestion is that unless the procedure is more fully considered as a social phenomenon, there is relatively little prospect of developing this particular way of treating human beings as sources of data.

The rationale of interviewing

The foundations of interviewing are to be found in the mundane observation that people can report on what they feel, tell others about aspects of their lives, disclose what their hopes and fears are, offer their opinions, state their beliefs, answer questions about who they see regularly, what they did last week, how much they spend on food, and so on; to put it simply, they can impart masses of information about themselves. The purpose of the interview is to make full and systematic use of this fact to gather data for research purposes. And, in its way, this relatively unremarkable fact about human beings has, in the hands of skilled researchers, created a most remarkable instrument of social research. Using as data what the respondent says about himself or herself potentially offers the social researcher access to vast storehouses of information. The social researcher is not limited to what he or she can immediately perceive or experience, but is able to cover as many dimensions of as many people as resources permit. The social researcher is not limited to studying fairly small groups of people, as is the case with participant observation, but can potentially investigate many thousands of people. Nor is the researcher limited to interviewing only members of his own society, but can interview people in other societies and, moreover, people who may be illiterate and, therefore, leave no written records of their social activities. In short, by using verbal reports offered by respondents, the investigator has access to an almost infinite variety of information that would be virtually impossible to gather by any other method. Moreover, such reports, when analysed using the various methods of statistical treatments available to survey researchers, can be used, so it is claimed, to describe or explain fundamental features of society, its nature, and changes to which it might be subject.

Now we can begin to see more clearly some of the instrumental presuppositions upon which the interview method depends. For one, the method is predicated on the claim that answers offered by a respondent to questions proffered by an interviewer are valid indicators of whatever aspects of the respondent's social life and being that are the subject of investigation. That is, to put it at its most basic, that the respondent is at least an adequate reporter of his or her attitudes, beliefs, and other subjective states, can inform the investigator of the nature of his or her relationships with others, and report on behaviour both in the past and intended. For another. and related to the first presupposition we have just highlighted, the interview makes use of a model of the social actor that makes a clear distinction between observable and reportable social behaviour and the various internal states of mind that accompany and may even cause or predispose that social behaviour. But, as far as the interview is concerned, access to both of these is through the answers offered by the respondent to carefully constructed and systematically administered questions. As we shall see later in this chapter, neither of these presuppositions are as straightforward as they may first appear.

Types of interview

The most common criterion for classifying interviews is in terms of their degree of standardisation; that is, according to the extent to which the interviewer is allowed to vary both the content and the order of questions asked. At one extreme is the structured type in which the interviewer uses a schedule to which he, or she, must rigidly adhere for all respondents alike. The same questions and the order in which they appear on the schedule would be administered, in a survey, to all respondents by all interviewers in the same way. The justification for this form of interviewing is that of standardising stimuli. That is, in an effort to ensure that any variations in the replies respondents give to questions are genuine variations and not due to idiosyncrasies arising from variations in the form of the questions and their placement in the interview, each respondent should be given, as far as it is possible, the same question in the same serial order. Thus, if an interviewer were to ask some questions of a respondent in one way and then vary them for another respondent, he or she could not be sure what effect this variation in the administration of the question had on the replies received. Further, it could be that a question asked early in an interview affects answers to subsequent questions and if this order were to be altered in any way it becomes, as in the previous example, difficult to detect the effect this might have on the replies. Of course, it is necessary to assume that the questions, however they are phrased, are understood in the same way by all the respondents whatever differences they might have in education, sex, and so on. Unless all respondents share a single interpretation of a question their answers cannot be compared.

However, there is a place in social research, and an important one at that, for the type of interview which stands at the other extreme to the structured one, and this is filled by the non-standardised interview. In this type the interviewer works from a list indicating, often in some detail, the kind of topics to be covered in the interview. The interviewer is free to ask questions in whatever way he, or she, thinks appropriate and natural, and in whatever order felt to be most effective in the circumstances. Both the interviewer and the respondent are allowed much greater leeway in asking and answering questions than is the case with the structured interview. Such an interview almost amounts to a conversation. Flexibility is the keynote and is a characteristic argued to be especially welcome in pilot studies preliminary to a full-scale study. It allows researchers to test out various lines of questioning, try out different ways of phrasing questions, gauge the tenor of likely replies, and so on. In addition to this use, the non-standardised interview is very often used when interviewing key personnel in an organisation when richer and fuller material is required.

The focused interview is closely related to the non-standardised or unstructured interview, and differs mainly in the extent to which the direction of the interview is controlled by the interviewer.[3]

Between the two extremes of standardised and non-standardised interviews is the rather large category of semi-structured interviews. As their name suggests they combine, or attempt to do so, the advantages of both of the two polar types just discussed. The interviewer normally has to ask specified questions but is free to probe beyond them as necessary. The relative weighting of standardised and non-standardised items can vary from research to research. The most common arrangement is to use the standardised format for 'face sheet' information, such as the age, sex, marital status, educational history of the respondent, and other relevant data of a demographic character. The less standardised section is used to elicit information more varied and qualitative in character.

Each type of interview is designed to achieve a particular research task. The non-standardised interview, it is argued, is most suitably used in exploratory studies where little of any systematic nature is known about the subject. In studies such as these a researcher might interview a small group of people in a fairly free-ranging manner with the intention of gaining useful guidance for the construction of more systematic and standard-ised interview schedules. The researcher will be looking for indications of the salience of topics, the extent to which questions are understood by different classes of respondents, the likely range of replies to given questions, and so on. These pilot studies are often of immense value in the design of more systematic and more extensive social surveys.

This type of interview is also used as an adjunct to a wider sample survey to provide illustrative material in the form of extended statements given by respondents who are taken to typify particular classes of subjects. This kind of data helps to 'fill out' the bare bones of responses given to highly standardised questions. In studies of organisations, such as factories and other business enterprises, and public offices, this form of interviewing is often reserved for key personnel while the larger-scale interviewing of other members of the organisation is done by means of a more standardised schedule.

There is a limit to which the non-standardised interview can be used with larger samples. It is extremely costly in terms of research time and money since such interviewing can easily take up to two hours or more. Moreover, the data produced are by no means easy to code and analyse. In fact, pilot studies using the non-standardised format are a useful guide to the coding categories a researcher might use in a larger survey. Accordingly, where large samples are necessary, the structured or semi-structured format gives a number of advantages. They are less costly in time and money to administer, are more straight-forward to code and process, and can be used by interviewers not necessarily fully conversant with all the fine details of the research aims. Further, the quantitative form in which the results of standardised interviews can be cast makes it especially important in the rigorous testing of hypotheses.

Question and questionnaire construction

What follows particularly applies to schedules or questionnaires used in standardised interviews, though they are points which need to be borne in mind in other types of interviewing. The first question a researcher needs to ask is what does he want to find out, and why? Whatever theoretical ideas inform the research, these will have to be translated into a question or statement form understandable to a relevant respondent. Especially useful here is information and experience gained from a pilot study. It is little use asking a respondent if he feels 'socially integrated' or whether his life is characterised by 'anomie'. Concepts such as these will need to be transformed into some readily understandable questions or statements which serve as indices of these more abstract and theoretical concepts.

Apart from the content of the questionnaire items decisions will have to be made on the form of the question-and-answer unit. Basically there are two choices here, between 'open-ended' and 'closed' or 'fixed-alternatives' questions.

The 'fixed-alternatives' question, as its name suggests, provides the respondent with a selection of answers, 'yes', or 'no', or 'don't know' being the simplest, from which he or she has to make an appropriate choice. In some cases such multiple-choice items form attitude scales in which each alternative is given a numerical weighting so that a set of such items can be cumulated to give the respondent an overall score on the scale. For example, a questionnaire designed to investigate attitudes towards work may provide respondents with a list of statements indicating a point of view to which he or she has to express a level of agreement or disagreement (see Table 1). Depending on the particular dimension being measured, the degree of agreement may be given a high weighting and that of disagreement a lower weighting. A scale like this will normally consist of a series of such statements tapping the same attitudinal dimension. The cumulated score over all statements constituting a particular scale provides the researcher with a quantitative means of describing respondents in terms of their scores which can be correlated with other variables of interest to the research.[4]

TABLE 1

'Most of the time I find my work fulfilling'				
STRONGLY AGREE	AGREE	UNDECIDED	DISAGREE	STRONGLY DISAGREE

The 'open-ended' item allows the respondent the freedom to provide an answer in whatever form he or she chooses. For example, 'What do you think about the first year of the Thatcher government?' or, 'What do you think about those British athletes who are going to compete in the Moscow Olympics?' Unlike 'fixed-alternative' items, the coding categories of 'open-ended' items usually have to be decided after the interviewing stage of the research is complete in order to see the kind of responses produced by the question. It also takes longer to ask open-ended questions and record the responses. However, it is possible that the richness of the replies is well worth this cost. It is not unusual for questionnaires to contain a mixture of both types of question. In the main, open-ended questions are best used, it is suggested, in the following circumstances: exploratory surveys when a researcher needs to elicit the respondent's frame of reference without prompting; helping to sustain *rapport*; and, finally, to encourage the respondent's thinking in a certain area.[5]

The wording of questions is as important as the form. A question should be precise and free of ambiguity. Each question should, for example, express a single idea. A question such as, 'Should Britain spend less on defence and more on education?' requires a single response, agreement or disagreement, yet any particular respondent could be of the view that the country should spend more on both or less on both. The question, in other words, is confusing and any answer possibly ambiguous. Loaded questions should be avoided, although in statements comprising attitude scales points of view have of necessity to be expressed. In these cases respondents reply to the loading by expressing their degree of acceptance. Questions should be as short as is feasible, be easily understood, and avoid esoteric language. They should be specific about events or topics; for example, instead of asking, 'How often have you been off work?' ask, 'How many times in the past two months have you been off work for whatever reason?' In this way a standardised frame is provided for all respondents alike making comparisons meaningful. In phrasing questions it is as well to remember to protect the self-esteem of the subject by avoiding subtle hints as to what an appropriate or desirable answer might be. Also, it is necessary to avoid giving the impression that the respondent's answers are in any way exceptional no matter how hair-raising. In the case of fixed-alternative questions the alternatives provided should be exhaustive covering all possible ranges of response including 'don't know' or 'no answer', and be mutually exclusive.[6]

The order of questions is another matter which needs careful attention. Early questions may predispose answers to later ones. A technique known as 'funnelling' can be useful in guiding the interviewer through the schedule and in encouraging the respondent to give fuller answers. General questions on some relevant theme are followed by some specific ones. Using this mode of question organisation, a respondent and interviewer can often be guided through subsets of questions. For example, some questions may be relevant only to married women, so an initial question about marital status is asked, followed by an instruction for those who have answered in a particular way to move on to the relevant subset.

Sequencing questions can play a vital role in easing the respondent into the interview. Uncontroversial and fairly routine questions – not always easy to spot – should normally come at the beginning, leaving personal and intimate ones for later. By then the interviewer and respondent will, hopefully, have established *rapport*. Closing the interview can be eased by using less challenging questions.

One final point as far as the design of questionnaires is concerned. An interview can last anything from 15 minutes to a few hours, so it is essential to maintain the informant's interest and attention for the duration. This means that the designer must avoid long sequences of questions demanding little thought or deliberation by the respondent, otherwise the respondent is likely to grow bored and provide ill-considered answers in a desire to terminate the interview as quickly as possible. This can be serious in the case of attitude scales where respondents by simply offering the same answer to the series of items produce a 'response set' distorting the eventual score. Earlier it was suggested that the judicious use of 'open-ended' questions can go some way to mitigating these effects by making the questionnaire more varied and interesting. But the designer must not go too far in the other direction by filling the questionnaire with deeply sensitive and thought-provoking questions so that the informant is exhausted after a few minutes. Many of these difficulties can be anticipated and corrected by testing the questionnaire in field conditions prior to the full-scale study.

The process of interviewing

Although the interview, in some form or another, has been a data collection instrument from the earliest empirical researches, the main development over the years 'has been the increasing systematisation of the interview techniques'.[7] The early interviews were rarely deliberately engineered and designed encounters. These days, however, there is considerable body of lore concerning interviewing method and its application.

A fact mostly ignored but which is none the less important to note about most data collection methods used in the social sciences is that they involve the researcher in social encounters with his or her subjects: the interview is no different in this. Indeed, the validity of the interview, it is argued, depends upon the effective establishment of a particular kind of social relationship between the interviewer and the respondent. The task of the interviewer is to obtain information, often of a highly personal and private nature, from a respondent who is a stranger and has little obligation to spend time and effort answering questions. A respondent is free to refuse to give an interview or to break off at any moment. Nor is there any guarantee that the respondent will tell the truth or furnish any information required in all its fullness. To avoid all of these, and more, pitfalls the interviewer must be exceedingly careful, and in training manuals a great deal of effort is devoted to proper and effective interview behaviour.

A number of stages in the interview-respondent relationship can be distinguished. The first stage of contact is especially crucial. Obviously if this fails there will be no interview. Getting respondents to consent to an interview is not always a simple matter. Appointments made over the telephone are relatively easy to refuse or break. Personal contact is much better but by no means foolproof. At the outset, the interviewer must ensure the co-operation of the intended respondent. This means that the interviewer must quickly establish a legitimacy in the eyes of the putative respondent. Academic researchers are not the only ones to use the interview. It is also used by pollsters, government researchers, market researchers, and as a cover for some sales pitch, and people differ in their estimations of the utility of these varied uses to which the interview can be put. As far as academic research is concerned there is only one rule for the interviewer: honesty. This may not necessarily result in a higher rate of acceptances, but is required if only to show respect for one's subject. The interviewer must give the respondent sufficient information about who the interviewer is, why he is there, how the respondent came to be selected for interview, what the questions will be about, assurances given as to the confidentiality of replies, and permission sought for the interview to take place. Any form of bullying is out.

If all this results in an interview being granted, the next stage requires the interviewer to establish a suitable relationship with the respondent: one normally described as a relationship with good *rapport*. The interviewer must communicate trust, reassurance, and likeableness to the respondent in order to maintain his or her interest and motivation in the continuance of the interview. Interviewers should never threaten respondents or destroy their confidence in the relationship. Many manuals for interviewers recommend that they use friendly small talk to ease the situation a little before embarking on the interview proper. Benney and Hughes, in discussing the 'behavioural conventions' of interviewing, refer to the norm of 'equality' which should govern interviewer-respondent relations.[8] 'Equality' assumes that information is more likely to be valid if freely given. Therefore, from the outset the interview should be a relationship freely entered into by both parties, but especially by the respondent. Benney and Hughes liken it to a contractual relationship such that for allowing the interviewer to direct the relationship the respondent 'is assured that he will not meet with denial, contradiction, competition, or other harassment. As with all contractual relations, the fiction or convention of equality must govern the situation.'[9] This means, too, that the interviewer should try to minimise any inequalities of age, sex, intelligence, social status, expertness, and so forth, which may exist between the interviewer and the informant. Clearly, it is not always easy to adhere to this convention.

What happens in detail during the interview stage itself will, of course, vary with circumstance and the type of interview schedule being used. If the interview is non-standardised or contains a significant number of non-standardised elements the interviewer should aim to relax the respondent as soon as possible so that he or she feels free enough to talk at some length. It is also a good idea to ask relatively innocuous questions early so that both parties can become used to each other more quickly. If, on the other hand, the interviewing method is the standardised type, while every effort should be made to relax the respondent the questions should be administered in the form and in the order set out. In this case the second convention suggested by Benney and Hughes, 'comparability' becomes especially pertinent. This convention is designed to minimise the immediate and unique features of a particular interview encounter so that only those aspects which are generalisable across interviews remain salient. In this way what the interviewer receives from the respondent as answers are treated as variables about social properties, rather than as details about a particular person in a particular social encounter. None the less, it is important in both types of interview that the interviewer treat each encounter as a separate experience to guard against the surreptitious influence of prejudgements about typical responses.[10]

A major goal of the interview is to gather relevant replies to the questions asked. Accordingly, an interviewer must be quick to recognise whether an answer is adequate given the question's objective, and must be ready to probe or encourage the respondent to elaborate or reformulate an answer. This might amount to a simple, 'Yes, I see', or 'That's interesting', but may require a more standard probe of the kind, 'Could you be a little more specific about that?' or, 'What do you mean by that, exactly?' These must be offered in a friendly and reassuring way without threatening the respondent or implying that he or she is a fool or dullard. Among the most difficult responses to cope with are 'don't know' ones. Such an answer might imply genuine ignorance, that the respondent does not understand the question asked, is embarrassed by an answer that might be given, or any number of things. Only delicate probing can illuminate such an answer further. In some cases interviewers are instructed on how many and what types of probes to use with particular questions.

Of course, all of these efforts will be wasted if the interviewer fails to record the answers as they are given. With the structured type of questionnaire the interviewer has to make sure that the category given is correctly and clearly marked. With open-ended questions all the words spoken must be recorded, avoiding paraphrase or précis.

The final stage arrives when the interview itself is complete and it is time for the interviewer to disengage from the scene. This can often be harder than it looks, especially if the relationship has been a rewarding one for the respondent. Although many people, initially, express a reluctance to be interviewed, once they begin this reluctance often disappears making it harder for the interviewer to keep within reasonable time limits. Nor is this too difficult to understand. The interviewer is giving the respondent a chance to talk anonymously without fear of contradiction, signs of boredom, disagreement, disapproval, and so on, often about deeply personal matters; a temptation few of us would be able to resist. Accordingly, disengagement may have to be delicately handled. What must be avoided at all costs is giving the respondent the impression that now the interviewer has got what he came for he no longer cares overmuch and all he wants to do is leave and on to the next. A good compromise is to be fairly businesslike or professional in one's attitude, stressing the value of the interview to the research, thanking the respondent for all his time and effort, and politely withdrawing from the encounter. Abruptness needs to be avoided except in the direst of emergencies!

Interviewing is not an easy matter. It can often be a harrowing and frustrating experience; reasons perhaps why academic researchers, funds permitting, are increasingly making use of professional interviewers provided by suitably accredited agencies. Training can certainly improve success rates and increase efficiency; especially important where large samples of people have to be interviewed. One salutary study reinforcing this point is reported by Hyman.[11] Fifteen people were ostensibly hired for a special study, even though they had little or no experience of interviewing. Each was sent to interview a series of people, among them 'planted' respondents: one, a 'punctilious liberal' who simply would not give unqualified responses; another was a 'hostile bigot' who proved to be unfriendly, aggressive, highly suspicious, and rude; and, finally, an 'alternative respondent' who offered himself or herself in place of the respondent who was not, at that time, available. Interspersed among the plants were uncoached respondents. The interviews with the plants were secretly recorded. Errors of various kinds were found. For example, confronted with the 'hostile bigot' some interviewers, not perhaps surprisingly, did not ask a large number of questions, hoping, no doubt, to terminate the interview as quickly as possible. A typical error was to record answers consistently with other answers the respondent had provided, even though the particular answer given was ambiguous. Instead of probing further the interviewers tended to reinterpret the question in terms of what they expected it to be. These and other errors illustrate some of the difficulties facing even trained interviewers in the face of less than ideal respondents.

The conventions of interviewing and the establishment of an effective relationship between interviewer and respondent are only part of the story. Equally important are the questions asked since the entire enterprise of interviewing depends upon these verbal stimuli eliciting replies which constitute data the interview is designed to collect. For this reason the design of the questions and the interview schedule is crucial.

Evaluation of the interview

The aim of the interview is to obtain information from a respondent. Clearly, to be of any use for social research the interviewer must be confident that this information is accurate. It is to achieve this end that all the conventions of interviewing and questionnaire design are devised. It is known that people can lie, say things intended to maximise their self-esteem, try to avoid offending others, and so on. All of these, and more, can lead to bias in the information gathered. An early study by Edwards, for example, found that the 'social desirability' variable affected responses to questions.[12] Personality traits judged desirable in others were more likely to find their way into self-ratings than were items judged to be less desirable. A similar finding appears in a study concerned with the relationship between social class and ethnicity on mental health, in which it is suggested that many of the responses about the prevalence of mental health symptoms reflect cultural differences in the social desirability of modes of expressing distress and willingness to report it. Puerto Ricans, to take one instance, regarded many of the items indicating mental distress as less desirable than did members of other ethnic groups.[13]

It is findings such as these which raise nagging doubts about the interview method. Although the interview would seem to offer many advantages to the researcher in that it substitutes what the respondent says about his or her behaviour for detailed and often arduous observation of actual behaviour, it is also a well-known fact of life that people often do not do what they say they will do, or have not done what they report they have done. Even with so-called straightforward factual questions about, for example, how people voted in a previous election, can produce errors of 20 per cent or more.[14] Nor are these difficult to understand. After all, the situations in which people find themselves often change in unanticipated ways, and whatever one might say in an interview isolated from those very processes which impinge on courses of action, it is another matter when one is confronted with situations which call for action. Thus, in an interview one might agree to all kinds of high-minded principles only to find oneself providing excuses or justifications when confronted by a conflict between self-interest and principle. In light of this it is perhaps not so surprising to find widespread condemnation of trade unions among the very people who are just as likely to come out on strike when their wages are at issue as are those who do not express such condemnation. Or to find large sections of the population expressing sentiments in favour of racial equality, but agreeing with immigration controls especially when there is the threat to employment.

Before becoming too cynical about the level of principled behaviour among the British population, we do need to look rather closer at what these comments might imply about the interview itself. Clearly, the point is not simply that people are often inconsistent as between what they say and what they do, but whether the relationship between saying or doing, to put it this way, is adequately conceptualised in the presuppositions of the interview method itself. The potential offered by the interview in allowing a researcher to cover a wide range of topics, to explore the past, present, and intended behaviour of respondents depends upon the respondent being truthful in what he or she reports. It implies, too, that the respondent is a good predictor of what he or she will do, whether this be voting for a particular political party in an imminent election, buying a particular brand of soap powder, or whatever. Or, to be slightly more sophisticated, it assumes that data gathered in the interview on matters such as attitudes are adequate predictors of relevant behaviours, For example, whether a worker who scores high on a scale measuring dissatisfaction with his work will be likely to be absent from work more than those who score low, be readier to go on strike, complain about management more, and so on. Yet, as we have already suggested, there is no firm guarantee that any of these assumptions hold. After all, people are routinely forgetful, try to put themselves in as favourable a light as possible, and, no matter how well intentioned, fail to carry out what they intend to do.

As we have seen, researchers have not been unaware of these kinds of problems as all the efforts devoted to questionnaire design, interviewing styles, and the study of interviewer effects suggest. One of the biggest problems arises from the fact that the interview is an occasion isolated from most of the matters it concerns itself with, namely, the social behaviour of the respondent. The interview is isolated in at least two senses: from the respondent's past and from the future. With regard to the past the problem for the researcher is to assess how much of what is reported by the respondent is refracted through the lens of the present. The isolation from the future creates different problems no less intractable. To repeat a point made earlier, though a respondent may express strong support for all kinds of sentiments in the comfort of an interview, when actually confronted with situations where these sentiments may have relevance, he or she is no longer isolated from all the factors which impinge on behaviour and, accordingly, may well act in ways, 'inconsistent' with beliefs or attitudes expressed in the interview. This particular observation should be no surprise to social scientists in view of their strong theoretical commitment to the notion that social behaviour is governed, to a large degree, by various social structural constraints not always perceived by social actors themselves.

What should be obvious by now is the intimacy with which these issues are bound up with important theoretical problems in the social sciences, and illustrates once again how instrumental presuppostions are closely interwoven with these theoretical ones. The interview is a social encounter and, as researchers have shown, cannot be exempted from normal social processes that govern such encounters. This is why such stress is laid on interviewing and questionnaire techniques and the management by the interviewer of the interviewer-respondent relationship. What is being claimed here is that a particular kind of social relationship is likely to result in more adequate and truthful replies. However, we are suggesting that the model informing the interviewer might well not be consistent with the kind of models the data produced are designed to illuminate or establish. There are so many facets to this issue that it is impossible to deal with them all except in general terms, and in such terms it can be stated as follows: to what extent can a researcher generalise from data gathered in an interview to social behaviour and processes outside it?[15] One can look at the problem as one of licensing various interpretations based on data collected from a social situation which we have already suggested is both isolated and artificial.

The strategy that has been followed for many years is to refine the method and techniques of the interview to improve its validity and reliability.[16] The methods we discussed earlier represent only a small part of the lore of interviewing practice developed over the years precisely in response to the difficulties we are highlighting here. Especially important in this connection is the question of the instrumental effectiveness of the interview relationship. For one thing it is not self-evident that the establishment of a 'warm and trusting' relationship will get the respondent to tell the truth as best he or she can. It seems plausible to argue that it could, just as likely, result in the respondent avoiding potential controversy, offering instead blandness, and deceptions designed to maintain conviviality.[17] Certainly few police interrogators or even job-selection interviewers would necessarily subscribe to the methods proposed by social research interviewers as the best method for getting at the truth. Even in social research other interview relationships have been used. Kinsey, for example, in his studies of human sexual behaviour, used the model of the prosecuting lawyer rather than that of the faceless and inoffensive social researcher. By all accounts his strict, direct, and aggressive manner seemed to work.[18]

The point is, of course, that the procedures of interviewing are as much infused with ethical sensibilities as they are with instrumental concerns. While academic social researchers do not need licences to ply their trade, public opinion would be grievously offended, and rightly so, if interviewers were to appear on a respondent's doorstep at 8.00 a.m. backed by five or six 'heavies', threatening dire consequences for the respondent's family and career if he does not agree to co-operate and answer a few questions. Though this example might appear rather fanciful, it does suggest that the interview method of data collection, and some of the instrumental presuppositions on which it is based, derive their plausibility from what we might refer to as wider cultural conventions. One can put this fairly strongly by claiming that the interview, as a method of social research, depends very heavily upon particular cultural conventions prevalent in some kinds of social system. It presupposes, for example, a fairly stable social and political order in which the majority of the potential respondent population do not feel particularly intimidated by requests for interviews. Moreover, they must feel confident that their private remarks will not be disclosed to either the authorities or others who have no right to know what has transpired in a social research interview. To the extent to which conventions or norms such as these do not prevail within a society, or a group, then doubts will be raised about the ability of respondents to express themselves freely in an interview. Similarly, the interview itself, as a social relationship, depends on other cultural conceptions which give it legitimacy as a social encounter. It would be hard to imagine interviewing, for the purposes of social research, a Viking raider, or an Elizabethan soldier or, more contemporaneously, a Kalahari bushman or a Sicilian peasant. We are not saying that one could not interview respondents from these latter peoples but would suggest that, at least, they might find it difficult to see the point of an activity which presupposes a very different kind of social order; one in which literacy is common, personal viewpoints deemed significant, private lives investigated by duly authorised persons, extensive public accounting procedures, a stable population, and so on.[19]

None of this, of course, necessarily invalidates the interview method, except when it is used in societies or groups where the kind of cultural underpinnings we have just mentioned are absent. And, moreover, these are not always to be found in exotic and less developed regions of the world. In our own society it is not easy to interview tramps, meths drinkers, members of the IRA, or even the heads of large industries, senior civil servants, the leaders of political parties, and other holders of the élite positions. But, social scientists who use the interview are as aware of these kinds of factors as anyone else, and would be among the first to concede the general principle that any method of data collection has to be evaluated in terms of the general social conditions that prevail, as well as in terms of its methodological adequacy. Indeed, knowledge of the society and its culture is essential for an interviewer/researcher to evaluate how best to go about interviewing, how the effect of particular characteristics of the interviewer such as say, age and social class may be assessed, and so on. The convention of 'equality' by which the interviewer should try to minimise any inequalities arising from age, sex, ethnicity, social status, and so forth is not always easy to meet, yet it is more than useful to know how these social characteristics might affect responses from members of the researched population. What, for example, would be the 'interviewer effect' of using 'black' interviewers to interview immigrant populations in this country as opposed to using middle-class 'white' interviewers?[20] Does the topic of the interview matter? And so on. Questions such as these are not easy to answer, but what is more certain is that both the use of the method itself and an assessment of any 'interviewer effects' on responses presuppose a wide knowledge on the part of the researcher of the society and the culture in which the method is to be used.

Not surprisingly, much research has been done on the effects of interviewer characteristics on the interview situation and on the respondent. Interviewers, of course, cannot but influence respondents since people always react to characteristics they perceive in others. Among these characteristics are those especially salient in the culture or society concerned, as well as the omnirelevant features of gender, status, and age. In some societies, such as the United States, ethnicity must be counted among these. In 1968, just after the assassination of Martin Luther King, Schuman and Converse interviewed 619 black residents of Detroit, using a mix of black interviewers, mainly older women with experience as professional interviewers, and white, male and female, graduate students.[21] It was found that black and white interviewers obtained significantly different responses to over 25 per cent of the questions. Yet, perhaps more significantly, against expectations, some questions did not produce strong race-of-interviewer effect. In other words, the effects of race is not always in the direction that might be expected. That is, we cannot always assume that black respondents are more likely to tell the truth to black interviewers than they are to white. In this case, white respondents might distort their answers in a more integrationist and less racially hostile direction to please white interviewers, they may also express more militant sentiments to please black interviewers. It appears, too, that differences in response to the race of the interviewer were greater among the low-income and less educated respondents.

Among other interviewer characteristics, status has been found to have variable effects. In some cases, equivalence of social status can result in greater *rapport* but this does not always result in more truthful answers.[22] Once again, no coherent picture emerges from this research. Similarly, with respect to other interviewer characteristics, religion, sex, age, and so on, the effects are highly variable suggesting no simple rules whereby these factors can be controlled. Thus, it is by no means easy to meet the conventions of equality and comparability mentioned earlier.

A further twist to these particular issues is added when interviewing is used as part of cross-cultural studies, which have, in recent years, become more common. Here matters become more complicated by the fact that a researcher is not dealing with one culture but with two or more, which raises the possibility that the conventions governing all the aspects of the interview encounter will vary, often considerably. But not only is the interview itself affected, so, too, are the questions themselves. The researcher, in short, cannot assume that the same words and sentences mean the same thing in the different cultures even if, on the face of it, they speak the same language.[23] Deutscher uses, among others, the example of a common-or-garden word, 'friend'. The lexical equivalent in German is *Freund*, and is a term reserved for a few longstanding intimates, whereas the English 'friend' can be applied to a wider circle of acquaintances. None of these problems are insuperable, especially if the researchers remember that 'a vocabulary is not merely a string of words; immanent within it are societal textures'.[24] By careful translation by bilinguals many of these kinds of problems can be at least detected if not entirely eradicated. But more to the point here, once again, is that these efforts require knowledge, often of a detailed and precise kind, of the society and culture to be studied by the interview method.

Up to this point we have been talking about the biases that can arise from the interview itself, such as the various sorts of 'interviewer effects', the factors which encourage or discourage a respondent to be forthcoming, and so on, and have argued that by themselves none of these biases add up to a wholesale condemnation of the method. Quite the contrary. Over the years knowledge gained of the kind of biases that can affect responses has been used to improve interviewing technique and to evaluate the validity of results obtained.

However, this is by no means the whole of the story. So far we have been discussing the interview, and the problems which arise from it as an instrument of social research. But perhaps the discussion has been over-individualistic in the stance it has given to these problems. After all, an interview is normally part of a social survey inquiring into the beliefs, attitudes, relationships, etc. of collectivities of people, and it may be that this is the proper level to assess it. Thus, we should perhaps be less concerned whether a particular respondent acts in accordance with the views he or she expresses in an interview, but more with the extent to which the data reveal significant relationships with respect to the group as a whole. As the research accumulates more and more interview data, individual variations should cancel each other out if there is no systematic bias operating across all the interviews more or less equally. If this assumption is plausible all the researcher needs to do is search the data for significant patterns. For example, attitudinal data can be correlated with so-called structural variables, such as income, lifestyle, age, occupation, social mobility, and so forth, and if there are systematic and significant differences between subgroups, then this would seem to lend strength to the validity of the data collection method. Pollsters at election times do reasonably well on the whole, predicting the outcomes of elections by relying on sufficiently large representative samples. Some of those interviewed may change their minds, even at the last minute, may not even vote at all, may even lie about their intentions, but in the aggregate, such actions tend to cancel each other out to provide a reasonably accurate estimate of the result.[25] But, of course, it can be argued that election prediction is not an appropriate model for the kinds of social scientific research which make use of the interview.

Indeed, the strategy just mentioned is little more than a practical manoeuvre to get around awkward questions to do with the interview itself. And, up to a point they can work, if only as solutions to limited and very practical problems. However, we began this evaluation of the interview by posing the problem as one of licensing inferences from data gathered in the interview to what we might bluntly term 'real life' social processes. The matters of bias are important here, but there are other important dimensions to consider too. The methods of good interviewing recommended by practitioners can be seen as devices to encourage the respondent to speak authentically. By this we point to the interpersonal tactics designed to get the respondent to say what he, or she, truly feels or believes about certain things, accurately report on things done, relationships entered into, and so on. This is essential if the verbal data collected in the interview are to be regarded as an adequate substitute for actual observation of the subject over a long period of time. But, even if the interviewer has performed magnificently and is convinced that the data he has obtained are as authentic as possible, there still remains the question of the relationship between this interview encounter and what we earlier called 'real life social processes'. Deutscher refers to this matter as the relationship between 'words' and 'deeds' and remarks that

one of the more regretful consequences of our neglect of the relationship between words and deeds has been the development of a technology which is inappropriate to the understanding of human behaviour, and, conversely, the almost complete absence of a technology which can facilitate our learning about the conditions under which people in various categories do or do not 'put their monies where their mouths are'.[26]

Deutscher is largely noting here an oft-remarked-on discrepancy we referred to earlier between attitudes and behaviour. However, there is another way of looking at this problem which does not rely on cynically charging large segments of the population with inconsistency or the lack of moral fibre.

To examine this other way we need to remind ourselves of the processes of designing an interview schedule, the techniques of interviewing itself and, in so doing, we will try to bring together a number of themes raised in the earlier discussion. In designing an interview schedule we remarked that the researcher has to choose between a standardised format or a non-standardised one, or some mixture of the two. In making this choice a number of considerations will, no doubt, be deemed relevant: ratio of interviewers to sample size, cost, methods of data analysis; nature of the sample population; knowledge already available; whether the research is mainly exploratory or hypothesis-testing; and so on. But whatever the eventual choice made, this will place a heavy constraint on the interview and the sense made of the respondent's replies. If the researcher decides to use mainly fixed choice items in an effort to standardise stimuli across interviews this will, inevitably, restrict the ability of the interviewer and the informant to amplify responses. This does not merely imply a sacrifice of richness and it can be misleading. Though respondents can and often do answer questions given to them in terms of categories provided, this is not the same thing as saying that these categories adequately reflect the respondent's meaning. What, for example, would we infer about a respondent who replied 'AGREE' to the question in Table 1? The question itself asks about 'most times' (and questions such as those are by no means rare in questionnaires), but how does the interviewer know what 'most times' means here? Is X's reply equivalent to Y's who also chose the AGREE response?[27] The point is that the structure of the question format imposes a version of meaning, or set of criteria, to assess the respondent's replies that may or may not equate with the meaning the respondent would wish, in other circumstances, to subscribe to. Nor is there any guarantee that the stimuli offered to respondents in the various interviews are interpreted in the same way by all. No matter how the interviewer tries to play the role prescribed for him or her by all the training manuals, the respondent also brings expectations of various kinds to the interview encounter and it is not known in advance what these might be. For these reasons it is hard quite to see in what ways the use of standardised stimuli in the form of prestructured questions, standarised behaviour on the part of the interviewer, and so on, can result in a set of interviews equivalent in all respects, and the researcher has no business treating them as if they were.

Suppose, on the other hand, the researcher decides to use open-ended questions. The immediate consequence of this is that richness is gained at the expense of comparability; or, at least, on the face of it it looks this way. But this may be a large gain. Certainly it would seem to avoid some of the pitfalls mentioned in the last paragraph in connection with standardised schedules. The interviewer can probe replies which are unclear, ask for clarifications, pursue interesting matters in more depth, and so on. The point about this procedure is when does one stop probing? At the time when both interviewer and respondent collapse exhausted on the floor? When the interviewer is satisfied that no gain is to be made by pursuing matters further? Or when the respondent says 'stop'? What is reasonably certain is that any suggested stopping-points will vary between interviews. Moreover, who decides what replies need further probing? Presumably this responsibility devolves on the interviewer who will have to decide on the spot whether a particular reply is unclear, worthy of elaboration, or whatever.

What, hopefully, we are beginning to see here are more of the consequences of treating the interview as a social encounter in all its particularities and complexities. This is not simply a matter of the interview drawing upon wide cultural conventions of the kind we mentioned earlier in this chapter, but of its being a face-to-face encounter with all the immediacy that this implies. Furthermore, it is this quality of the interview which gives rise to the methodological dilemmas reflected in the choice between a standardised versus an open-ended format; the choice, to put it in other ways, between generality and richness, or between reliability and validity.[28] Errors, it is claimed, arise because the researcher and the actual questions are both potentially misinterpreted and misinterpreting. The efforts to maximise reliability result in standardised methods which, it could be argued, seriously misinterpret the respondent's meaning by imposing an artificial structure by means of the methods employed to elicit those very meanings.[29] In other words, what is being employed here are social scientists' versions of meaning, adequacy, and so forth. Indeed, the notion of 'bias' implies a standard to use in judging the truth or the authenticity of replies; but whose standard? On the other hand, efforts to maximise richness seriously militate against the purpose of the interview survey by emphasising the particularities of each interview encounter. The proponents of the interview method have devoted their energies to trying to develop ways of compromising between these two alternatives. But, we must ask, is this possible?

At bottom, of course, this is a theoretical question every bit as much as it is a question of method. What is being argued here is that the interview tradition embodies an inadequate theory of social action which, among other things, ignores the way in which meanings are created and used in social situations. In terms of a model used in Chapter 2, the interview method presupposes that words uttered by a respondent in an interview could stand as indicators of both inner thoughts, such things as beliefs, attitudes, or opinions, and social acts. However, as we have seen, the relationship between those various elements is not as simple as one might suppose. The attempts to remove biases which can arise as a result of the profound social character of the interview encounter are, in part, a recognition of this complexity. But to speak of 'biases' is to presume that the task of the interviewer is to get as close as possible to what the truth of the matter is: whether it be what the respondent truly feels, what he has in fact done, who in fact he is associated with, and what he will truthfully do. If, however, we look at this from another sociological tradition, the achievement of this task becomes much more problematical than simply making a list of contaminants which interfere with the attainment of some ideal interview. The symbolic interactionists, for example, argue that social action is symbolic in nature, being a response to the meanings embedded in particular situations. The interview is a social situation to which both parties bring expectancies, presuppositions, beliefs, experiences, etc. and without understanding these we shall be unable to understand the social dynamics of interview encounters. And here we are not speaking of interviews in general, but very much in particular. In other words, we cannot presuppose that a particular interviewing style will work with all respondents alike. We cannot assume that what appear from our point of view to be inconsistent responses are, in fact, inconsistent from the respondent's point of view. We cannot afford to prejudge the question of whether standardised items are, in fact, treated in the same way by all respondents. We cannot assume that similar responses necessarily mean the same thing, and so on.

Conclusion

This discussion of the interview method has taken us to the point where we must look again at the instrumental presuppositions on which the method is based as sociological theories proposing specific models of the social actor and society. That is, the prescription for good interviewing should be read as a set of propositions on how the interviewer and the respondent should interact to achieve the aims of scientifically collecting verbal data. This is important because it is these models which, in effect, license the inferences that are drawn from data gathered in the interview. And, it may be that the supposed findings of interview-based research owe much more to these models than they do to the power of the method to get 'at the facts'. If, of course, the models are to be found defective, then doubt must be cast on the data produced by the method.

Whether or not we have reached this stage is up to the reader to decide in the light of these and other arguments. But we can go a little further along the road. In discussing the survey we remarked, following Galtung, that the survey contains presuppositions which may well be peculiar to one type of society.[30] We are thinking here especially of its democratic and individualistic flavour. Much the same points can be made about interviewing. Indeed, we suggest that many of the instrumental and theoretical presuppositions of the interview derive, in no small measure, from wider cultural and moral conventions. Here we can point to the recommendations contained in many manuals about the most effective method of establishing a suitable relationship between the interviewer and the respondent. As we suggested earlier, it is by no means self-evident that good *rapport* necessarily results in more valid data. Indeed, there is some evidence to suggest that this can result in various kinds of misrepresentation. Converse and Schuman indicate that the current advice given to interviewers at the Institute of Social Research, Michigan, lays less stress on *rapport* and more on a professional, more impersonal, approach.[31] But whether this mode of behaviour is more effective is, in a way, beside the point. Perhaps more important is the implicit model of the social actor which underlies it, and the consequences this has for judgements of bias, misrepresentation, and so forth. There seems little doubt that underlying many of the prescriptions recommended for interviewers is a model of the ideal respondent and the typical social actor which constitutes the yardstick against which actual respondents can be evaluated. Such an ideal respondent would express himself or herself clearly and unequivocally, be honest and truthful in replies, respond sympathetically to the interviewer's interpersonal tactics, express little in the way of prejudiced or bigoted opinions, is a person who truly perceives the nature of the world in which he or she lives, would not unduly respond to the idiosyncrasies and artificiality of the interview situation itself, and so on. In other words, he or she sees the social world much as the social scientist sees it, and any departure from this ideal is a source of flawed perception, bias, and untruth. Such a model, we would suggest, squares little with the model of the social actor presupposed in many social scientific theories. For example, as we mentioned in connection with the survey, most social scientific theories recognise that the actor is located in many relationships which affect not only his or her behaviour but also his or her attitudes, beliefs, and the way the world is cognitively and symbolically structured. Instead, what most of the instrumental prescriptions of interviewing presume is a social actor who conforms, dare we say it, to the ideal of the rational liberal-democratic individual: one, moreover, who is, in the interview at least, detached from the society in which he or she lives. An individual who is in, but not of, the society.

All of this is not offered particularly by way of condemnation of the interview method, but is addressing the question of what conclusions the researcher is licensed to draw from the data so produced. In this the social scientist has the choice of a large number of social theories, not all of which are consistent with the orthodox presuppositions of the interview which we discussed earlier in the chapter. Take the issue of meaning, for example. Validity of the interview method depends on a meaning equivalence being established between what the researcher intends by a question or an item and the way in which it is understood by the respondent. The same goes for the respondent's answer, namely, that it is understood by the interviewer in the way intended by the interviewee. However, Freudian theories, for example, would certainly question the simple-mindedness of this view. Alternatively, those social theories which see meaning as very much a situated matter would also baulk at this claim.

To put it bluntly, what interviewing tries to achieve is a situation and mode of relationship in which the words offered by the respondent in response to questions put by the interviewer, are treatable as 'scientific data'. In this respect, the social situation that is the interview is privileged compared with other situations in which the individual may find himself or herself. Whether or not this argument is justified is another matter, but it does raise some awkward questions.

The interviewer is not interested in the interview itself. To use an image of Mehan and Wood, the interview as part of a survey dips into everyday life and takes 'a reading as if people were oil in an engine and the interview a calibrated dipstick'.[32] The researcher assumes that what sticks to the dipstick is not important of itself except for what it indicates about something else. The data produced, the answers to questions or items, are not treated as the outcome of a particular interaction but stand on behalf of, or index, other activities that the researcher never observes. As we said right at the beginning of this chapter, rather than look at activities, the researcher-interviewer accepts the descriptions offered by the respondent as indicators of the activities themselves.[33] But such descriptions are always a gloss for the behaviour; a gloss, moreover, very much guided by the interviewer. Guided so that the respondent feels at ease, will tell the truth, and frame replies so that they fit into the researcher's categories; categories normally established prior to the research itself. Cicourel's study of interviewing is especially revealing here.[34] His detailed study shows how 'taken-for-granted' interpersonal knowledge is used by interviewers in order to 'get the work done'. But, while such knowledge is rarely explicitly stated, it is essential to the production of the 'facts' revealed in the tabular presentation that is the end result of the research. In other words, a great deal of interpretative work is necessary on the part of both the interviewer and the respondent in order to generate 'appropriate' responses. Yet this interpretative work is neither part of the researcher's theory nor method. Indeed, one inevitable tension here is between the goals of the researcher as researcher and the demands of polite discourse. The interviewer cannot escape from the difficulties of everyday life interpretations and actions. The ways of common sense thus compromise literal hypothesis-testing, yet they are necessary conditions for eliciting the desired data.[35] As Mehan and Wood conclude:

The interview situation is a chunk of time from one reality that is separate from the lived reality ... which the interview is presumed to index. The interview's purpose is to capture lived experience outside the interview. Yet, the interview itself is a new experience only vaguely related to the experiences it is supposed to represent. Even when the interviewer and respondent share the same reality – in the sense of 'class' background, language, age – distortion is inevitable.[36]

The point is, to use Benney and Hughes' terms, that the conventions of interviewing, namely comparability and equality, have to be achieved on each interviewing occasion. Yet, little in fact is known about interviewer-respondent interactions, apart from the work of Cicourel and, earlier, Hyman. What is known suggests that the interpersonal tactics, necessary in any social encounter, are extremely varied; so varied that one finds it difficult, without further evidence, to meet the essential conventions. The interview prescriptions we discussed earlier seem to presume what they should investigate.

Some of the themes and issues we have raised will be discussed again in Chapters 5 and 6. Now we wish to turn to another method of data collection, participant observation, which represents another tradition of social research though, as we shall see, efforts have been made to regard it as simply another technique of investigation among others. As we shall see, this claim is not easy to sustain. Instead, what we have is a method which presupposes a particular version of the social actor and society; a version which is, in many ways, radically different from those normally presupposed by the survey and interviewing method.

5

PARTICIPANT OBSERVATION

Although today among the least frequently used of the methods of data collection available to social scientists, something approximating to participant observation has been in use from time immemorial. An early example might be travellers' tales of their experiences and life in foreign lands; a tradition preserved in more refined form in social anthropology. It is also a method of which we all, as members of society, have experience, at least in the sense that the study of groups in which one interacts is an integral part of ordinary life.[1] Of course, as a practice in social research, it aims to go beyond our taken-for-granted social competences. Nevertheless, there are common elements in the skills and knowledge required for ordinary interaction and participant observation. Participant observation, as its name implies, requires the investigator to involve himself or herself in the lives of those being studied, and so involves a number of activities including looking, listening, enquiring, and recording. Although participation may involve encounters similar in scope and intention to the interviewing associated with the survey, it cannot be disassembled into a series of discrete practices following a logical sequence. In contrast to survey method, participant observation involves the engagement of the researcher in a series of ordinary social situations as an ordinary human being. As Becker and Geer define it, participant observation is that 'method in which the observer participates in the daily life of the people under study, either openly in the role of researcher or covertly in some disguised role'.[2] We might compare this with a situation in which human subjects are simply observed, as in the case of laboratory experiments, where a researcher is concealed behind a screen of one-way glass.[3] The participant observer on the other hand, normally takes on a role which can credibly be accommodated in the social group or organisation being studied. As we shall see later in this chapter, this is sometimes a matter of fine judgement. But the aim of the practice is to build up, over a period of time, an account of the situation being studied which takes the views of the participants in the situation very seriously indeed. In short, the researcher tries to obtain an 'insider's' view of the social group.

Some form of participation and observation has recurrently been used in social research. Charles Booth, for example, lived for a period among the poor so that he could better understand the lives they led.[4] Although the earliest works in anthropology relied on the reported experiences of explorers and colonial administrators,[5] modern anthropology has developed methods of immediate observation to a high art. A major early study which extols the virtues of participant observation is B. Malinowski's study, *Argonauts of the Western Pacific*, published in 1922.[6] No doubt in sharp reaction to the early practice of relying on vicarious accounts of primitive tribes, Malinowski elaborates the many advantages of participant observation. Though he did not use the term to describe his method of research, his book is a powerful statement of the advantages of direct observation. The primitive tribes he and other anthropologists have studied do not, in the main, possess written records. Accordingly, any sociological account of these societies must be based on what the members of such societies do, and how they interact with each other in the present. By trying to see the world from the natives' point of view, so holding in abeyance the preconceptions natural in his own society, the investigator can better identify the relationships, rules, and values which constitute the core processes of society. However, although the initial reasons for direct observation are similar in some respects in both anthropology and sociology, they involve differences of emphasis and practice. For one thing, the anthropologist could seldom plausibly adopt the role of another participant, as sociologists commonly do by becoming bread delivery salesmen, or machine-operators,[7] so passing as an ordinary member of the social group they are investigating. For the anthropologist, adopting some sort of

'outsider's' role is usually inevitable. But the differences between anthropological and sociological uses of participant observation do not turn on accidental factors like these. Actually,
similar methods of data collection have become part and parcel
of very different theoretical approaches to social life and have
rather different emphases and characteristics as a result. For
many years, roughly the period 1920 to 1950, anthropology in
the West was dominated by a structural–functional approach to
the analysis of society. Different institutions and primary groups
were seen as having a function within the general structure of
society, and the anthropological recommendations about the use
of direct observation in data collection reflect this.[8] As we shall
see in this chapter, however, the framework of ideas within
which the practice of participant observation was developed in
sociology, and which participant observation studies helped to
extend, was quite different. In a very real sense, the sociological
and anthropological uses of participation are two rather different
theory-specific methods. In the remainder of this chapter we
shall focus exclusively on the sociological use of participant
observation.

The origin and rationale of participant observation

The early development of participant observation was pioneered
in Chicago in the 1920s and 1930s as a result of the urging of
Robert Park, Ernest Burgess, and W. I. Thomas.[9] The city of
Chicago at this time was growing rapidly and changing very
dramatically, presenting many examples of dynamic social
change. At the University of Chicago, sociology had been taught
from before the turn of the century, and was by this time firmly
institutionalised. In the early decades of the century the
sociological work done there had been primarily conceptual,
analytic, and speculative. Small had pioneered theoretical
analysis of society; Dewey had reorientated psychology towards
the analysis of interaction and communication; and Cooley, at
nearby Michigan, developed a powerful conceptualisation of
institutions.[10] Park, Burgess, and Thomas represent a second
wave of sociologists at Chicago, concerned to couple theoretical
speculation with empirical study. The changing milieux of

Chicago at the time, accommodating wave after wave of immi-
grants, and developing as a major manufacturing and processing
centre for the Middle West must have seemed a challenging
prospect for sociological study.

But the roots of these sociologists' interest in the subjects they
studied, and in the way they went about their work, are not to
be found solely in the social situation of Chicago itself. They lie
deeper, and must in part be explained in terms of the general
ideas and motivations of early sociologists. In a similar way to
our discussion of the early developments of the survey in Chapter 3, it is appropriate to trace the effect which the general social
context had on the development of participant observation as a
method of research. In a remarkable way, the development of
sociology in America can be seen as paralleling the development
of sociology in Britain. The early history of sociology in America
can be written in terms of a transition from economic liberalism
to a more general and social liberalism. This is a major theme of
two important studies of the development of sociology in the
USA.[11] This change is certainly reflected in the work done at
Chicago in the period under review. Spencer's ideas, which
embodied the idea of economic competitiveness, indeed made it
central to social progress, had found powerful advocates in
America, most importantly W. G. Sumner.[12] The extent to
which social progress was a natural outcome of economic
development, as Sumner proposed, can be seen as a continuing
and underlying theme in much of the early sociological writing
produced in America. A similar preoccupation runs through the
work of the second generation of scholars in Chicago who first
undertook sustained empirical study in the city. The extent to
which the little communities springing up in Chicago at the time
were to be regarded as 'natural' communities, social entities
which were self-regulating and not in need of imposed control, is
a continuing preoccupation of these scholars.

To the American mind the small community was the natural
unit of social organisation. It is important to note, as C. W.
Mills points out, that many of the important contributors to the
debate about social pathology begun in America at this time,
were born and raised in small towns.[13] This probably helped to
shape the way in which culturally and occupationally distinctive

areas, which were a feature of all the developing American cities at the time, were thought about. The slums, the rooming-house districts, even the delinquent groups of the city, tended to be measured implicitly against the standard of 'natural' community. Rock writes that each of the areas studied by the sociologists '. . . was treated as a symbolic world which created and perpetuated a distinctive moral and social organisation. Each was subjected to interpretive analysis which attempted to reproduce the processes by which that organisation was brought into being.'[14] Rock also suggests that comparison was frequently drawn between these 'natural' processes and structures and 'those structures produced by planning and science'.[15] If we add to this concern with the minutiae of change in the community, American pragmatism, with its disdain for highly rationalistic and formalised theories and its preference for first-hand practical knowledge, two important ingredients of the motivation towards detailed participative social study come together. These traits are important intellectual components of the context in which the early participant studies were completed. Anderson's study of the 'hobo' was one of the first of these published in 1923; it was followed by Thrasher and his study of gangs, Cressey and his study of 'taxi dance halls', and many more.[16] At this time too, Lindeman's study of method, which makes first use of the term 'participant observation' was published.[17]

The development and use of participant observation as a method of data collection can be divided into three stages. Firstly, the stage which we have already described in which the method was crystallised out as a means of extending sociological enquiry. This covers the period from 1920 or so until the middle or late 1930s. Overlapping with this and extending well into the postwar period, we have a stage in which there were sustained attempts to develop the method, to articulate its applications and justifications fully. In this stage the theoretical underpinnings of the method were fully developed and it was detached from the analysis of social ecology in the context of which, as we have seen, it was first used. The sociological theory it came to be closely associated with is known as symbolic interactionism. Though the founding statements of this set of ideas were also made in the early years of this century, they were powerfully developed during the 1920s by G. H. Mead and his followers. From the late 1920s, method and theory began to be unified in the work of W. F. Whyte, Everett Hughes, and H. S. Becker. While a student at Harvard, Whyte conducted a seminal study of an Italian community in a slum area of Boston. He later joined the faculty at Chicago and conducted a series of valued studies of industry.[18] Hughes, also at Chicago, refined participant observation as a method for the study of occupational groups, and sent out a succession of gifted students to study occupations in like manner. In a series of papers he then attempted to unify and codify their findings to draw more general sociological lessons.[19] Becker, Goffman, and others found a whole series of wider applications for the theory and method, so laying the foundation for the modern study of deviancy and social process within institutions at the same time.[20] More clearly than is the case with orthodox social science, the practitioners of symbolic interaction and participation can be seen to retain their interest in social reform, its desirability and likely success.

While this style of analysis and research continues to be influential, if peripheral, in social science, there are grounds for thinking that a third stage in the development of participant observation has been entered into. And, though we shall not say very much about this, it is clear that the method has not escaped criticism or attempts to explore the implications of the theoretical and other assumptions implicit in the method, and so to produce new, more searching methods of social investigation. However, in this chapter, we shall be primarily concerned with the second of these stages of development, in which participant observation was most fully developed and used, and in which the uses and implications of the method were carefully set out. In the remainder of this chapter we shall consider three aspects of participant observation developed by its practitioners. Firstly, the research process of participant observation, emphasising the stress placed on the production of social knowledge. Secondly, we shall consider the problems in the use of participant observation identified by these writers themselves. Finally, we shall consider the connection between participant observation and its underlying theory.

The research process of participant observation

When it was first used, participant observation was seen as one important strategy in the social scientist's armoury, to be selected on mainly instrumental grounds. Similar suggestions have sometimes been made in texts on methods in more recent times.[21] Thus it was suggested that participant observation could be used to explore a group or social situation as a prelude to more formal methods of research, such as an interview survey, or as an extension of such a research programme. However, for the majority of the social scientists whose work we shall comment upon in this chapter, the choice of participant observation is more mandatory. Implicitly or explicitly, they claim that it is by far the most effective way, if not the only way, of investigating social organisation. This view is associated with a radical criticism of the methods we have discussed in previous chapters, namely the interview and social survey, and is a repudiation of the notion that the social sciences are scientific in the same manner as the natural sciences. It is a view which rejects the quantitative stance of much of social science research in favour of one which stresses instead a more qualitative approach. The argument rests very much on the contention that social life is constructed in and through meanings which cannot be studied in terms of deterministic laws, but must be understood interpretively: a process made possibly only by some form of participation in, and experience of, that which is to be understood.

We have made the point that the method of participant observation is closely associated with a particular theoretical perspective in sociology; a perspective which stresses the interactive and negotiated character of the social order, created in and through the meanings actors use to make sense of and interpret the world in which they live. There is little sense here of an objective social structure of the kind presupposed by the early social surveyors. Instead, the social structure is seen as a multitude of scenic processes, constantly moving and changing as actors negotiate and renegotiate their course of action. There is little conception, too, of society as a macro-structure, and a preference for studying rather limited sections of visible social life: those groups and processes tangible and familiar to the actors concerned.

Such small-scale worlds, plus the injunction that the social investigator should examine them from the point of view of the participants themselves, provide the putative participant observer with the first of his, or her, problems; gaining access or entry. This is often a matter of fine judgement. One of the major arguments for participant observation is that it allows the study of persons and groups in their natural habitat as opposed to the artificial circumstances of the laboratory or the detached and often remote method of the survey interview. As a result, the researcher needs to enter the group or setting in such a way as to disturb as little as possible the lives of those being studied. To enter as a researcher may well generate 'reactive effects' and contaminate or disturb the very phenomenon in which he or she is interested. On the other hand, in the case of some groups, exclusive religious cults would be an example, it may be extremely difficult to enter at all even posing as a full-fledged member; certainly not without considerable Thespian talent and effort. However, in other cases there may be no role available other than that of researcher, due to the obvious ethnic differences between members of the target group and the researcher. Indeed, on occasion it may be that an 'outsider' role, such as that of researcher, is the appropriate one to adopt. Trice suggests, for example, that in cases where two or more groups confront each other, as did affiliates and non-affiliates to Alcoholics Anonymous in a state hospital he was studying, the subjects may invest an outsider with appropriate neutrality enabling the researcher to interact more satisfactorily with all parties instead of being regarded as a partisan.[22] Vidich goes further, arguing that to the extent to which an observer's data are conditioned by the subjects' response to his or her role, a 'stranger' has an important advantage. He or she can, with justification, maintain an attitude of *naïveté* and exploit the role of 'stranger' to the full. It would be relatively easy for such a researcher to break taboos, breach local custom, and so on, and still maintain a tenable position. Such an investigator can ask questions in the naïve way not possible within his or her own value assumptions.[23] The fieldworker can present himself 'as an interested incompetent who needs toleration and remedial instruction'.[24]

The general lesson in all this is that there are no hard-and-fast rules dictating what sort of role to adopt. In his early study, Whyte adopted the vague role of a writer concerned to write a history of 'Cornerville'. For his purposes this turned out to be an apposite choice. The inhabitants of Cornerville knew something about writers; though not a regular job in the usual sense it was respectable, was done by educated people, and, moreover, involved unconventional hours. Further, such a role gave Whyte a licence to ask questions without being deemed too inquisitive or nosey, since it was understood that writers needed to gather material.[25] In other cases nothing so beautifully ill-defined a role as a writer will do. One example at this other extreme is a study of the motivations and attitudes of enlisted men which required a researcher to 'enlist' as a basic trainee in order to become a full-fledged member of the group involved. His identity as a researcher was unknown, even to his commanding officer.[26] Since the observer was to enlist under an assumed name and remain in the group for a long period, an identity had to be constructed for him so that his false identity could be verified as 'true' if the necessity arose. So successful was the coaching he received as a putative member of the adolescent subculture that the recruiting sergeant at the post where he was to enlist recommended that he be rejected because, by all the evidence, he was a juvenile delinquent.

While not all participant observation studies necessitate such extreme identity creations, there are numerous examples of the considerable trouble researchers have gone to so that they may 'pass' within the group under investigation. It is worth noting, however, that Whyte, as have others, found that acceptance within the social groups in his district depended far more on the personal relationships he was able to develop than on any rationale or explanation of what he was doing. As long as he was able to win the support of key individuals he was fairly confident that he could obtain what he wanted from other members of the group he approached.

I soon found that people were developing their own explanation about me: I was writing a book about Cornerville. This might seem entirely too vague an explanation, and yet it sufficed. I found that my acceptance in the district depended on the personal relationships I developed far more than upon any explanation I might give. ... If I was all right, then my project was all right; if I was no good, then no amount of explanation could convince them that the book was a good idea.[27]

Nor should it be forgotten that any fieldworker, whether participant observer or not, is fitted into a role by the people he is studying, and inevitably there will be variations from field situation to field situation in the identity assignments given to fieldworkers. In the normal anthropological field situation, for example, the researcher is often identified as a trader, missionary, district officer, or any other role with which the native population is familiar.[28] Such identities may well affect the access to information and generally play a part in the data the researcher is able to gather.

Four roles open to the participant observer have been identified.[29] The first, the 'complete participant', is that role in which the researcher becomes a full-fledged member of the group under study, any research purpose being concealed. A major feature of this role is the large degree of pretence. The second role is that of 'participant-as-observer' in which both researcher and subjects are aware of the fact that theirs is a fieldwork relationship. Good examples of this type of role are the numerous community studies in which the observer develops contacts and enduring relationships with individuals in the community. Since the research purpose is not concealed it is much easier for the fieldworker to use other techniques of data collection, including formal interviewing. 'Observer-as-participant' is the third role and, properly speaking, does not belong to strategy of research usually meant by participant observation since involvement with subjects is deliberately kept to a minimum. Typical of this research role is the one-visit interview. Similarly, the fourth role, 'complete observer', requires the investigator to insulate himself or herself from any social contact whatsoever with subjects. We are concerned with the first two roles mentioned.

Although the choice of participant role can often require courage, matters usually boil down to a careful weighing of the nature of the group, its accessibility and openness, research exigencies such as time and other resources, as well as the personal qualities of the researcher. However, one possibility needs to be anticipated which could arguably affect the objectivity of the research. Earlier it was pointed out that one of the major justifications for the research strategy of participant observation was that it enables a researcher to gain an 'insider's' view of the social world through participation in the way of life being studied. One danger of this is that the participant observer may become so much a participant that he or she is no longer capable of maintaining the role of researcher and becomes instead a full-fledged participant; a process aptly, if bluntly, called 'going native'. The role of participant observer not only includes the role selected best to gain entry and acceptance within the group concerned but also that of researcher; a dual emphasis that it is a matter of nice, often difficult, balance. If the observer errs too much on the side of researcher he or she will run the risk of exposure which, at the very least, could mean the ruin of the research and the waste of considerable effort or, at worst, more serious consequences better not contemplated. If the balance tips too far in the other direction the risk is a different one, namely, becoming so immersed in the group that it is impossible even to pretend to any detachment or objective observation.

These and similar risks vary according to the participant role adopted. Since that of 'complete participant' involves the most pretence it would seem to incur the greater risks. Gold puts the problem dramatically enough:

> The complete participant realizes that he, and he alone, knows that in reality he is other than the person he pretends to be. He must pretend that his real self is represented by the role, or roles, he plays in and out of the ... situation in relationships with people who, to him, are but informants. ... He must bind the mask of pretence to himself or stand the risk of exposure or failure.[30]

Thus, the 'complete participant' faces two day-to-day problems: first, becoming so self-conscious about not revealing his true identity that his observation is severely handicapped by attempting to give a convincing performance; second, becoming so immersed in the role he or she has chosen that the 'native' view is adopted entirely. In the case of 'participant-as-observer' the risks of immersion are still there but, obviously, since the research role is visible the problem of concealing this does not arise. But, as Vidich has noted, being both a participant and an observer is the 'strategy of having one's cake and eating it too.

Deceiving the society to study it and wooing the society to live in it.' The researcher's position is always ambivalent and remains marginal to the group or organisation being studied.[31] As we shall see later in this chapter, there are ethical considerations which are relevant here.

There are a number of strategies that have been used to cope with the often excruciating ambiguities built into the participant observer role. In the study of motivations and attitudes of enlisted men mentioned earlier, the observer was given every opportunity to report back to the research group, to disengage himself, even if only for a short time, in order to maintain the necessary balance of commitments. Irrespective of the research role adopted the researcher does need to find time for reflection and seclusion in order to write up field notes. The observer must always remember that there will come a time when he or she must disengage from the group and report any findings back to colleagues. Problems of detachment versus involvement will generally become more severe the longer the observer stays within the group unless satisfactory arrangements have been made to reinforce the research side of the role.

Once entry to the target group has been achieved the observer's next task is to make full use of the role selected in order to gather data relevant to the research purpose. It is at this time that all the personal qualities and skills of watching, listening, questioning, sociability, shrewdness, recollection, and so on, will have to be used to collect the data required.

An essential tool in the participant observer's craft is a field notebook in which everything felt to be relevant can be noted down. At first such notes may look little more than random jottings of odd remarks, notes of an unusual occurrence, a pet name, a tentative sociogram, vague but suggestive analyses, and so on. The main problem in the early stages of the research will be deciding what not to record, since until a plausible scheme of interpretation has emerged it will be hard to judge the relevance of anything. The temptation to record anything and everything will be hard to resist. Once again Whyte's experience is instructive here. He kept copious notes. Although for much of the time he was hanging around street corners, he would go to his room periodically to write up his observations. Most of his mornings were spent recording what had happened the day before. In the beginning these notes were kept chronologically, but this soon became unmanageable. His choice then was whether to file his material under topics, such as politics, the family, church and religious affairs, rackets, and so on, or to file according to the group he was with at the time. At this stage it became clear to him that it was the groups who were crucial to his conceptualisation, so he decided to file by this principle.

This also illustrates an important feature of participant observation, namely, the way in which the analysis of data accompanies the process of data collection itself, or, as Becker terms it, 'sequentially'.[32] Becker goes on to identify four main stages of analysis in participant observation research: the selection, identification, and definition of problems, concepts, and indices; the estimation of the distribution of phenomena; the incorporation of the findings into a model of the group, community, or organisation under study; and, finally, the presentation of evidence and proof. It is important to note that the first three of these stages are carried out while the fieldwork is in progress and form an integral part of that fieldwork. This pattern of working is not typical of other methods of data collection used in the social sciences.

During the first stage of identifying problems, concepts, and indices, a stage upon which the remainder depend, the observer looks for concepts that offer the greatest promise in yielding fruitful and interesting findings. Although a researcher may note that such-and-such occurred in a certain place at a particular time, this will remain an isolated and uninteresting finding unless it is placed within the context of some theory and its importance determined. An observer might notice, for example, that in a work group when a particular foreman appears the workers display an exaggerated involvement in their work tasks, relaxing the moment the foreman goes away. This may suggest something about the nature of the relationship between foreman and workers derived from the context of work itself or, alternatively, it may simply be the response of this group of workers to this foreman. By appropriate questioning and continued observation the researcher can begin to develop specific and more firmly drawn hypotheses about interaction in such a setting.

Initially, then, the observer will use data mainly to speculate about possibilities and, very important, to direct future observation. In terms of the example just used, the observer will need to look for other modes of behaviour which may throw light on the relationship between foremen and workers, and for other instances which may illuminate the kind of authority relationships that holds between them. Further observations may, of course, force the researcher to discard a number of provisional hypotheses. In addition, the researcher can make use of a number of principles to evaluate individual items of data. Statements by informants can be judged for their credibility. Has this informant got a particular axe to grind? Does the informant have reason to lie or otherwise embroider the truth? Did the informant actually witness the event being reported? Was the statement volunteered? Does the pattern of behaviour occur repeatedly? Is it done jokingly, insultingly, or merely for effect? And so on. Important here, too, is the relationship between observer and informant. If the researcher is a 'complete participant' he or she has to evaluate whether the role being played, whatever it might be, affects the behaviour observed or the statements offered. If, on the other hand, the researcher is playing the role of 'participant-as-observer' then it might be that the observer aspect of the role results in behaviour on the part of informants which would not naturally occur. This latter possibility can work both ways. A subject may say something or act when alone with the observer in ways which accurately reflect his or her perspective, but which could be inhibited by the presence of other subjects. However, the contrary to this is also possible, especially when the presence of others may give support to the expression of one's perspective. The manner in which the observer's role is itself defined is important here, although it is not always easy to gauge its effects.

None of the above problems have solutions which can be reduced to some technical routine. Instead, all rely on the judgement of the observer: a judgement based on long and intimate involvement with the ways of a group.

The next stage of research suggested by Becker, one not sharply distinguishable either analytically or temporally from the first, is discovering which of the many provisional hypotheses, problems, or ideas are worth pursuing as major elements of the study. In part, this is done by checking if the events or phenomena that prompted the initial hunch are widespread or typical within the group. This will almost certainly require collating various kinds of evidence about the group from many different sources, informants, observations, and so on. Normally because of the practical difficulties inherent in fieldwork, judgements about the frequency or the typicality of some event, pattern, of behaviour, or perspective, will not be quantitative in nature. None the less, estimations of likelihood are possible.

Becker's final stage of analysis in the fieldwork consists of incorporating particular findings into some generalised model of the group or organisation as a social system. Essentially this amounts to designing a descriptive model which best explains the data the researcher has assembled. The most common kinds of conclusions to emerge at this stage include: statements about the necessary and sufficient conditions for the existence of some phenomenon; statements that some phenomenon is 'basic' to the group or organisation in question, and, identification of a situation as an instance of some process identified in sociological theory. Once again it is important to note that this stage is a major part of the fieldwork. Preliminary models are refined by searching for possible negative cases so that the researcher can refine the model even more. The construction of such models, partial as they may be at times, is an operation very closely connected to the observer's techniques and interests at the time of fieldwork. Of course, more systematic working-out of the models must await a time when the observer can disengage from the fieldwork. This brings us to Becker's last stage, namely, the final analysis and the presentation of results.

This final stage consists of rechecking and refining models as carefully as possible. With the practical difficulties of fieldwork behind them, researchers can look over their material to take account of all information to assess the accuracy and plausibility of any conclusions. Models can be built more systematically, hypotheses subjected to even stricter tests, and interconnections formed into an overall synthesis.

An important consideration is the presentation of conclusions and evidence either for a research report or publication. In contrast to quantitative research, qualitative data and the inferences drawn from them are difficult to present succinctly. The highly systematised methods of quantitative social science, such as tabular presentation of statistical data, the use of measures of association, correlations, and so forth, permit highly formalised presentations in ways not open to the participant observer. Such qualitative material will normally consist of many different kinds of observations that are not simply categorised without using much of their value as data. Yet, a highly conscientious presentation of all the evidence will quite probably bore a reader or bury him in a surfeit of information. Becker's suggested solution to this particular problem is to present conclusions in the form of a natural history 'presenting the evidence as it came to the attention of the observer during the successive stages of his conceptualisation of the problem. . . . In this way, evidence is assessed as the substantive analysis is presented.'[33] This, he claims, would give any reader the opportunity to make his or her own judgement as to the adequacy of the research and the degree of confidence to attach to any conclusions.

Problems of participant observation

While passionately defended by its supporters, it should be no surprise to find that participant observation is also heavily criticised, especially by those who subscribe to the view that the social sciences should strive to emulate the natural sciences. For these the method relies far too heavily on unsystematic techniques of data collection, leaves too much to the whims of a single researcher, and fails even to approximate to the canons of objectivity and validity required by an effective science. Let us examine some of these criticisms more closely.

One of the major justifications of participant observation is that it enables a researcher to study a group in its natural setting and, moreover, to study the group for far longer and in more depth than is possible with the survey or any other research strategy. However, it can be objected that by taking a role the researcher may well affect the structure of the interactions being studied. This kind of 'control' or 'reactive' effect is common even in more formalised research methods such as the experiment, and is by no means a peculiar problem with participant observation.[34] Problems arise when it is unintentional or unforeseen affecting the research in unknown ways. Were Whyte's street-corner gangs unaffected by his presence? Is a company of recruits with a disguised officer in their midst the same as a group without such a researcher?

It is not only the group itself which may be affected by the researcher. The researcher, too, may be affected by his participation in the group. This may happen in a number of ways. For example, taking a role within a group tends to impose restrictions on a fuller understanding of any situation as it might appear from a differently located role. Further, as Whyte found out, as a researcher matures into a role his perception is likely to become more inflexible which will not only affect access to information but represent a reduced willingness to entertain alternative hypotheses and schemes of interpretation. He remarks that as he became part of the community and his data increased in richness, he found himself tending 'to take for granted the sort of behaviour that is taken for granted by the people I was observing'.[35] This process of 'maturation' can also affect subjects. The persons studied by the participant observer, whatever role is adopted, are of two major types: respondent and informant. An informant, like Doc in Whyte's study, has a special relationship with the researcher; there is normally a bond of trust between them, he gives information freely, explains what is going on, and so on. The informant becomes more like a colleague to the researcher and the relationship can develop into one of special intimacy. On the other hand, the respondent does not have this kind of relationship of special intimacy. Normally there will be no special trust between the researcher and the respondent, no privileged information imparted by the latter, and questions answered only when asked. By contrast the informant acts as an observer for the researcher and as a means of access into the group under investigation. However, it is possible for the informant to develop too deep a commitment to the researcher and the aims of the study and, not to put too pejorative an emphasis on it, becomes over-enthusiastic in the provision of information.

Once again there are no hard-and-fast rules to counter these and similar objections. However, it is not as if participant observers are unaware of these problems, as Becker's recommendations presented earlier show. Indeed, Becker goes further and claims that the participant observer, more than any other type of social investigator, is better placed to appreciate these and similar problems,

because he operates, when gathering data, in a social context rich in cues and information of all kinds. Because he sees and hears the people he studies in many situations...he builds an ever growing fund of impressions, many of them at the subliminal level, which give him an extensive base for the interpretation and analytic use of any particular datum. The wealth of information and impression sensitises him to subtleties...and forces him to raise continually new and different questions, which he brings to and tries to answer in succeeding observations.[36]

Becker, however, represents a branch of the supporters of participant observation who wish to claim that it is a better method for achieving the goals of a science of social life than other methods. As we have already seen, he argues that it is possible to construct and test hypotheses using the method. Indeed, he claims that more than other methods of research it fulfils better the aim of sociology, originally formulated by Weber, of providing explanation at the level of meaning.[37] For many supporters of the method, then, participant observation as a method of data collection was not a crucial option but a necessary part of the development of sociological theory.

To try and catch the interpretative process by remaining aloof as a so-called 'objective' observer and refusing to take the role of the acting unit is to risk the worst kind of subjectivism – the objective observer is likely to fill in the process of interpretation with his own surmises in place of catching the process as it occurs in the experience of the acting unit which uses it.[38]

It is, none the less, undeniable that a great deal of interpretative work is necessary on the part of the participant observer to bring conclusions out of the data: work which is not part of any explicitly formalised procedure. Can, for example, a highly educated middle-class researcher really empathise and understand aspects of the lives of lower-class people? How far can a young, fresh-faced university-trained sociologist really empathise with drug addicts, hustlers, prostitutes, beggers and panhandlers, and other members of deviant sub-cultures, who seem to form much of the subject-matter of participant observation? Might not his or her own life experiences cause him to draw inferences from his observations that may be widely at variance with the sort of inferences drawn by the subjects themselves? As Schwarz and Schwarz note, a certain amount of 'retrospective reworking...goes on without the observer being aware of it. Rather than finding a simple and direct connection between the occurrence of the event and its representation as data, we discovered that our observation began to expand the longer we thought about it.'[39] These kinds of problems can be compounded by the kind of contacts a participant observer is able to make within a group and the relationships allowed to him or to her. Clearly, this will be determined in large part by the researcher's social characteristics and by the norms of the group involved. An example of this is Gans' *Urban Villagers*.[40] He points out that his observations were limited because of strict segregation between the sexes. At gatherings the men grouped themselves in the living-room while the women stayed in the kitchen. Men were distinctly uncomfortable in the presence of women. The overriding feeling was that if a man and a woman are alone sexual contact between them is unavoidable. In light of this state of affairs more of Gans' data was collected from men than women. In some societies, such as the United States, racial and ethnic barriers are often difficult to surmount. For this reason it is perhaps not surprising that participant observation studies of lower-status groups seem more frequent than do studies of higher-status groups. The powerful are less likely to be flattered by the attentions of a researcher than are the less powerful. Age, too, can affect the relationships a researcher is able to establish with group members. Lofland suggests that young people may, on the whole be more acceptable in fieldwork roles. He argues that since the participant observer must always be watching and asking questions, in most settings younger people can more easily be accepted as incompetents, as people who do not know all that much and, hence, will not be offended by being told 'obvious' things by members of the group.[41]

In sum, many of the researcher's social characteristics, such things as age, sex, social class background, ethnicity, and so forth, can crucially affect the relationships that he or she can develop and, in addition, affect the inferences the researcher draws from the data collected. Even the best fieldworkers are limited in the kinds of relationships they are able to develop, and by their social characteristics and the structure of the setting being studied.

We have already referred to the fact that participant observation puts the researcher into a strange setting with all the attendant difficulty this engenders. The research process itself, of necessity, isolates him from his usual social world. A new social world has to be mastered and in a way that maintains research objectives. A new social role must be established, one which allows freedoms not always open to group members. Many researchers report feelings of unease, to put it no stronger than this, about not being accepted by their hosts. None the less, even though such feelings may pass with experience, there is little doubt that the fieldwork role is an ambivalent one. Since the gathering of data is the major aim, personal sentiments must often be suppressed to avoid antagonising important sources of data. But, the general point is that unlike the other methods of data collection we have described, there are no clear rules to follow in doing fieldwork. Carefully and strictly formulated hypotheses are rarely the inspiration of the research. There is normally no question of carefully selecting samples, no statistical means for testing hypotheses, and so on.

All of this may well generate anxieties in the researcher concerning whether or not he or she is being objective, gathering the right kind of data, being in a position to witness everything of relevance, and so forth. It may be that in response to such feelings the researcher becomes over-reliant on the first people to come to his assistance, and, as a consequence, they exert undue influence on his perceptions and on his ability to effect good *rapport* with other subjects. It is possible that a fieldworker becomes so intent on developing good relationships that he loses his grasp on the fact that he is a researcher. Admittedly, an essential part of his task as participant observer is that he 'resocialises' himself through the experience of research itself.

But it can go too far. As Whyte reports: 'As I became accepted with the community, I found myself becoming almost a non-observing participant. I got the feel of life in Cornerville, but that meant that I got to take for granted the same things that my Cornerville friends took for granted. I was immersed in it, but I could as yet make little sense of it.'[42]

The extreme form of this, as we noted earlier, is 'going native'. While in its extreme form this is rare, and on those occasions not of interest since it is not likely to result in anything for sociological evaluation, it can, none the less, result in analyses which are almost wholly one-sided, even if sympathetic to the subjects being studied. This is not a question of deliberate distortion or deception, rather one of a natural sympathy which affects the analysis and must be evaluated.

These points concern the effect that the mode of research itself can have on the collection, interpretation, and analysis of data produced by the method. Another set of influences is less directly concerned with the fieldworker's perception and more to do with his, or her, effect on the group and its situation under investigation. Fieldwork takes place in naturally occurring settings and it requires no great leap of imagination to suspect that the researcher's presence may well alter in significant ways the situation being studied. As Doc, one of Whyte's informants said: 'You've slowed me up plenty since you've been down here. Now, when I do something, I have to think what Bill Whyte would want to know about it and how I can explain it.'[43] The manifold ways in which such effects can occur are difficult to summarise. However, it is worth noting that 'reactive affects' are not confined to participant observation studies. Laboratory experiments, surveys, interviews, etc. are all prone to such effects which is one reason why so much effort has been devoted to evaluating or eradicating them. To the extent that nearly all social science data collection techniques involve the creation of, or the participation in, social situations, we would expect such influences to be endemic. The problem is to account for them in order better to judge their effects. As far as participant observation is concerned, Becker, for one, argues that the method of participant observation is probably less prone to such unacknowledged influences than are other methods. Prolonged involvement in the scene, careful weighing of informants and information, rechecking, and so on, means that little will be hidden from the observer.[44] Some participant observers, however, regard the researcher's ability to influence the setting as a positive asset. Whyte, for example, helped to organise the gangs to make a protest about the lack of hot water in the district, with some success. However, this does conflict with the standard advice to fieldworkers which is not to take sides on issues affecting the subjects. The dangers of taking sides are obvious enough: it may cut the researcher off from what could be important aspects of group life, unduly influence a 'natural situation, and so on. Yet, sometimes such intervention can be valuable for the research in that it tests out ideas or hypotheses. Whyte's action was based on over three years of fieldwork with the gangs and, it is arguable, helped further his understanding of the structure and culture of such gangs.

The general point about all the foregoing is that a researcher cannot avoid having an influence on the setting being studied. And one can reasonably surmise that those influences will vary according to setting, type of participant role adopted, length of observation, and so on. But, and this is perhaps the major point to make, the object should be for the researcher to make informed judgements about how and to what extent such influences affect the data he is able to collect, the inferences he may make, and the ultimate analysis presented. Aside from those methodological points there are some ethical issues surrounding deliberate intervention which we shall return to towards the end of this chapter.

Apart from these general complaints about the effect of participant observation research itself, there are others which begin to undermine its theoretical value. It should be obvious by now that the participant observer does not produce data of the kind generated by the survey and the experiment. A fieldworker may spend months assessing subjects, talking and listening to them. Rarely do they systematically interview large representative samples. They do not control or manipulate their subjects for the purposes of testing causal hypotheses, nor do they normally make use of any statistical presentation of their data. Instead their raw data is likely to consist of a detailed set of field notes reporting observations, encounters, happenings, reflections, etc. The question is: what theoretical value does this kind of data possess?

The first point to make is that a participant observation study is not based on systematic sampling procedures. Normally, fieldworkers are able to develop contacts with only a small minority of people in a group or a community. Indeed, it is also likely that this small group of people will be unrepresentative of the whole. The nature of the method often requires that contacts be made through existing and established networks which may well bypass others. More than this, though, is whether the group studied is typical of other groups. Are Whyte's gangs typical of other urban gangs? Are they a phenomenon of a particular period or phase of urban growth and decline? And so on. The actual group or setting chosen by a fieldworker depends upon a number of contingencies, especially those to do with ease of access and entry. Often the researcher has little discretion about where he can do his fieldwork, and chance encounters often play an important part. Gans, for example, wanted to study a slum and the way of life of a low-income population.[45] He felt that he should study a white slum because it would be easier for a white researcher to gain access. The one he chose was facilitated by the fact that an already existing research project concerned with redevelopment of the area was willing to offer him a job. However, by the time he entered, redevelopment had caused many of its inhabitants to leave and those that were left were disproportionately older and, for personal and financial reasons, could not move. Accordingly, he ended up studying a single, working-class, Italian community at a particular time in its history, and one which had unique and perhaps atypical features. The question is, then, whether his analysis and description of family life in the area can be extended to other low-income areas?

For this reason, many fieldworkers are content to limit the scope of their generalisations and regard their research as exploratory and to be supplemented by further studies on the same or similar themes. However, it is worth noting that this problem, if it is a problem, of generalising from a single case is not unique to participant observation studies. Many surveyors, for example, sample particular cities, towns, organisations, factories, etc. But one supposed virtue of quantitative studies com- pared with participant observation research is the explicit way in which the results can be presented. Earlier we summarised Becker's recommendations on this matter, but there is no doubt that compared with the social surveyor and the experiments, more discretion is available to the fieldworker. He, or she, is not bound by rules of inference or evidence in the same way. Moreover, since field data come from many different situations in many different forms rather than as explicitly measured vari- ables, it is much more difficult for the observer to give a sys- tematic account of how such-and-such conclusion is warranted. As Becker admits, it would be ridiculous to present all the descriptive material necessary for a reader to make his or her own assessment of the data and any inferences drawn from it. He notes that: 'Participant observation... has not done well with this problem, and the full weight of evidence for conclu- sions and the processes by which they were reached are usually not presented, so that the reader finds it difficult to make his own assessment of them and must rely on his faith in the researcher.'[46] We have already seen how Becker recommends problems such as these be overcome. None the less, for many the reports of participant observation studies remain little better than good journalism or anecdotal accounts of life, usually the seamier side. In other words, certainly not scientific in the way required. However, for others all these criticisms we have just discussed are beside the point, despite the efforts of Becker and others to bring participant observation into the fold of respect- ably social scientific modes of research. Indeed, Becker more than anyone has attempted to meet many, and more, of the criticisms we have just mentioned. To see the other justification let us turn to the relationship between symbolic interactionism and the method of participant observation.

Participant observation and symbolic interactionism

Perhaps no other sociological theory is so closely associated with a particular research method than symbolic interactionism is with participant observation. Moreover, there is little doubt that the method, and to a lesser degree the theory, is only a peripheral research tool of sociology. Not surprisingly, perhaps, given the considerable demands, personal and intellectual, it places on the fieldworkers. Yet, as a research strategy it has grown from a special conception of sociological knowledge and, inevitably, society.[47] Indeed, symbolic interactionists insist that the current technological emphasis of most of sociological methodology has usurped the proper concerns of the discipline, namely, the nature of man, society, and knowledge. They stress, too, 'that the activity of research is itself a proper object of sociological inquiry. Research is not taken to be a disembodied agent of pure logic, but a social encounter.'[48]

Symbolic interactionists, by and large, reject efforts to create a science of sociology through formal, rigorous, deductive, causal, and quantitative models of inquiry. Indeed, they would on the whole argue that the method of participant observation itself is ineffable; beyond formal instruction and elucidation. Sociological knowledge and understanding cannot be acquired through methodological formulae but must be a result of being in the world: knowledge is the result of praxis. Efforts to reduce methodology to a routine mode of inquiry by defining concepts precisely, rigorously, and, if possible, quantitatively, merely serve to distort the social world in fundamental ways. Any hypotheses should develop out of ethnographic work and not before. Knowledge should be an emergent property of inquiry not predetermined by abstract and socially unengaged intellectualising. Concepts should merely 'sensitise' the sociologist, not blind him to the reality in which he is to become involved.[49] Understanding should flow from 'an ongoing exploration of society, it cannot be engendered by fixed schemes and carefully manufactured hypotheses'.[50]

Fairly obviously presupposed here is a very different conception of knowledge compared with the previous methods of data collection we have discussed. To put it simply, they presuppose that relatively precise and rigorous general theories could be developed to explain a durable social world. The way to attain this knowledge is by the application of proper methodological principles aimed at providing objective, detached, rigorously formulated facts or data. In an important way, and this constitutes one of the major criticisms made by the interactionist against such methodologies, it is not necessary for the researcher to experience in any way the world being investigated. Research is an anonymous enterprise; a matter of method rather than persons. For the symbolic interactionist, on the other hand, authentic knowledge is furnished by immediate experience, not by the application of a scientific method. Put this way, participant observation affords the symbolic interactionist with the only method of grasping social reality; a method, moreover, which cannot be reduced or communicated by way of a programme or set of techniques.

At this point we begin to confront some of the theoretical presuppositions of symbolic interactionism which are, as it were, built into the method of participant observation. The vision of social reality incorporated in the previous methods we have discussed, namely the survey and the interview, implies that it can only be known through the use of particular rationally developed methodologies which enable the user to 'discover' or 'unearth' facts in the form of data. Social reality is not obvious to either the lay persons who inhabit that reality or to the social scientists who investigate it. Indeed, social reality as it appears to the 'unscientific' observer may not furnish unaided knowledge of the real social processes at work. Observation of surface appearances cannot yield scientific knowledge of social reality. Thus, Marxism, structural–functionalism, conflict theory, psycho-analysis, and many more, presuppose or postulate underlying, deeper processes at work beneath the phenomenal world of appearances which must be uncovered through rigorous methodological and theoretical work. On the other hand, participant observation and symbolic interactionism attend to the visible social world in which 'interaction is defined as an order which is *sui generis*, not simply as the vehicle for the manifestation by the sovereign and deep structures of society'.[51] Moreover, as we have already pointed out, any attempt to study interaction with so-called 'scientific' methods merely serves to distort this phenomenal social world. The observable is social reality: it lies nowhere else. To quote Rock once again: 'Interactionism espouses participant observation because it is based on an epistemology that describes immediate experience as an irreducible reality.'[52]

This can be seen in the flavour of participant observation reports which often consist of long quotations from members of the group being studied, are full of intimate and minute details, replete with the language and expressions used by the members, contain little in the way of abstract reflection, heady theory, or statistically based arguments. Instead, the reader is given an overwhelming impression of access to the meaningful life of those studied: an insight into a microcosm organised and shaped by those who live within it. There is little, too, that we would regard as of a general theoretical nature, striving to reduce social life to a few laws or principles of social organisation and process. Instead, there is a stress on the immediate, the particular, and the unique. Of course, crucial in all this is the observer himself, who selects, interprets, and presents the world he has studied for our perusal. But, if we remind ourselves of the non-routine character of fieldwork, it appears that the observer has a great deal to do with the production of the reality being investigated. It is intimately his picture and no one else's. Knowledge of social life has to be knowledge grounded in direct experience of that life. This in one reason why fieldwork, unlike the other methods we have discussed, cannot be programmed. A full grasp of social reality can only arise from engaging in the social life itself. If this were not the case, sociology could rely on reason and observation alone; *participant* observation would be unnecessary.

Yet there is a crucial paradox in all this. If direct experience is necessary and, by implication, prestructured research distorting of social reality, what status, then, can be accorded the field-worker's own analysis? If, on the other hand, fieldwork is the only way to grasp social reality, what commonly accepted and grounded principles can we use to evaluate this grasp? It is these and similar questions which make the issue of 'going native' more than a matter of slight amusement. For in an important sense 'going native' would seem to be the only available public evidence that the fieldworker has successfully completed his, or her, research. As Vidich remarks: 'If the participant observer seeks genuine experiences, unqualifiedly immersing and committing himself in the group he is studying, it may become impossible for him to objectify his own experiences for research purposes. ... Anthropologists who have "gone native" are cases in point; some of them stop publishing entirely.'[53] And yet, in some formulations of symbolic interactionism 'going native' would seem to be an achievement, at least in the sense that the observer has become fully socialised into the group being investigated. In other words, he has fully grasped the life being investigated by becoming a member. He is no longer a 'stranger' or an 'incompetent'. It is for reasons such as these that a number of sociologists charge participant observation with not only being unscientific but also unsociological. It also gives us some understanding of the very real ambiguities which are built into the participant observer role. We spoke earlier in this chapter of the stratagems used to reinforce the research side of the role and the anxieties fieldworkers often report about their efforts. Marginality has to be a way of life for the participant observer. As Hughes observes: 'The unending dialectic between the role of members (participant) and stranger (observer and reporter) is essential to the very concept of fieldwork, and this all participant-observers have in common: they must develop a dialectic relationship between being researchers and being participants.'[54]

And here we have another paradox, one we have noted before. Participant observation becomes impossible if there is a full commitment to the participant role or to the observation role. Indeed, it can be argued that a tension between the two is crucial. Without marginality the world being observed would not become strange and interesting; it would cease or fail to be rendered problematic. Yet, this may well isolate the researcher from the sociological domain by inferring connections, themes, and so forth without adequate warrant – from a sociological point of view.

We have already discussed some of the strategies often employed to cope with this marginality, but one more comment is worth making. In some cases, marginality may be built into the situation being researched. Much of participant observation is used to study various deviant groups of which few, if any, sociological researchers have any prior experience. This may have the effect as noted by Rock:

The juxtaposition of familiarity with unfamiliarity may furnish a proper combination of phenomenological distance with interpretability. Deviant worlds are rarely so isolated that there is no common symbolic currency between them and the outside. They provide significant refractions of meaning which are both strange and intelligible. The courting of deviancy by many interactionists may lie in that unusually provocative quality of the rule-breaking episode'.[55]

Whatever the truth or merits of these points of view, there is no doubt that participant observation does represent a very different tradition of sociological inquiry and approach to data collection than either the survey or the interview. Its reliance on sociological knowledge interpreted as intimate experience of the social world especially, marks it off from these other methods. Data, if this is quite the correct term, emerge as a result of the fieldworker's engagements with social life. Moreover, such data are not so much the product of an accredited method which can be taught to other practitioners, used again and again, but the result of the interpersonal and face-to-face encounters the researcher has with his subjects. There is little sense, too, of knowledge produced in this way as being cumulative. The social world revealed through participant observation is a world of shifting microcosms, constantly being built and reassembled and only occasionally glimpsed through the efforts of fieldworkers. Society can only be shown, and not understood through abstract, reifying, and rationally conceived principles.

Conclusion

Although, as we showed at the beginning of this chapter, there have been attempts to make participant observation appear as simply another method in the armoury of sociological data collection techniques, a closer look at the theory which inspired the method suggests that it cannot be so conceived. Instead, what we have is not merely another method of data collection but a radically different way of conceptualising the social world and the knowledge to be gleaned from and of that world. The theory argues, as do others of course, that routine method cannot provide knowledge of the social reality since it distorts that reality. The method relies, too, on a personalised and subjective experience of the phenomena under investigation; experience which, in its very communication becomes merely a pale representation or description of the meaningful world it supposedly portrays.

To pursue these matters further would take us too far afield.[56] However, we would like to conclude with some remarks on the ethics of participant observation. In engaging in fieldwork, as we have noted, it is often the case that the observer must represent himself, or herself, as other than a researcher by adopting a role that is appropriate for entry into the group being studied. This inevitably involves a large degree of pretence. Even when the research role is explicit, interaction within the setting will have to involve the researcher in treating such interactions as other than authentic or what they seem. 'Friendship can become transformed into capital, personal revelation into data, and conflict into illumination.'[57] In other words, disguised or overt, the fieldworker's role changes the significance and the authenticity of the things that transpire in the setting. Civility and espousal of intimacy, for example, can become degraded by being used as tactics to encourage disclosure by subjects, and the relationship between the researcher and his subjects becomes a predatory one.[58] Erikson, for one, believes that these kind of fronts, inevitable as they are, 'compromises both the people who wear them and the people for whom they are worn, and in doing so, violates the terms of a contract which the sociologist should be ready to honour in his dealings with others'.[59] He argues that the act of entering a social situation on the basis of 'deliberate fraud may be painful to the people who are thereby misled' and disturbing 'by failing to understand the conditions of intimacy that prevail in the group he has tried to invade'. Sympathy for the people being studied is not enough, since, whether disguised or undisguised, the fieldworker has to make use of fronts for ends which have not been sought or anticipated by his subjects. The trust which binds people together and which is so much a taken-for-granted property of social life is betrayed since the observer's appearances are counterfeit. Sociological fieldwork becomes a form of espionage, exploiting by treating subjects instrumentally.[60]

This criticism can be overdrawn, especially if it singles out one participant observation as the only method guilty of misrepresentation. None the less, it does serve to remind us that, in general, social science research does have a special ethical relationship with its subject-matter. Other methods, it is true, do not meet these issues in quite the same form as participant observation, but they are present none the less. Respondents are not forced to spend time being interviewed, but they have little control over the ways in which the information is used. Further, as we saw in Chapter 4, various interpersonal strategies are recommended as ways of eliciting respondents' willingness to participate in the research, and to improve *rapport*. While there may be a difference in degree, it is difficult to see this as better or worse than the participant observer's use of personal fronts for instrumental ends. Though we do not offer this as an excuse or a justification, it is worth reminding ourselves that such strategies are part and parcel of everyday life, as Goffman has so eloquently shown us.[61]

It is hard to see quite what one's professional response to these kind of charges can be, except to stress, once again, the importance of treating subjects with respect and honouring their way of life. What this injunction enjoins us to do with respect to particular research methods is another matter, and difficult to decide in the abstract. What is perhaps more certain is that if participant observation is guilty of these charges so are other methods of research, though in different ways.

6

THE SOCIAL BASIS OF SOCIAL RESEARCH

In this final chapter we want to draw together, albeit briefly, some of the issues which have emerged in the preceding discussion. In doing so we will address the question of the relationship of data collection practices to conceptions of social scientific knowledge and its changing role within society. Once again we shall refer to the presuppositions involved in research methods and indicate how these are intimately linked not only to the theoretical imagery which infuse a discipline but also to the concerns and values of the wider society. We shall begin by sketching out some historical trends in the development of social science and its practice.

We alluded earlier to two developments in research methods: firstly, the trend toward the production of precisely formulated theories and, secondly, the growth in the technology of research methods, especially in statistical theory, mathematical models, and detailed formalisation of research procedures themselves. Both of these tendencies, we suggested, encourage a view of social science research methods as a technology largely shorn of intrinsic social significance or political relevance. These developments are not unconnected to wider social changes which, in turn, help us to see, and perhaps understand, the social context in which research methods are situated.

The social changes we wish to identify and emphasise in this respect are bureaucratisation and professionalisation. All industrial societies show a marked tendency to develop specialised institutions. Indeed, the process of industrialisation has been described by sociologists in precisely these terms. Very simply put, all non-industrial societies are characterised by a small number of relatively undifferentiated social groupings, such as the family and wider kin, age sets, small communities, and so on. By contrast, industrial societies are characterised by a large number of highly specialised organisations, economic, political, legal, educational, and so on. Within them, personal, affective, and intimate relationships tend to be displaced by more impersonal, instrumental, and specialised ones. The precise causes and character of these changes cannot be adequately discussed here, although a good deal of social science may be seen as attempting to explain and illuminate them. Suffice it to say at this point that the differentiation of economic institutions which occurs with industrialisation is closely followed by considerable secondary differentiation of the wider institutional infrastructure, particularly in the organisation of the political system, especially the state. These developments have frequently been referred to as 'bureaucratisation', because the typical organisational form such institutions take is bureaucratic.

In most industrial countries, including Eastern European, social science has become institutionalised and, at least in part, a close associate of the bureaucratically organised state.[1] We have already referred to this tendency in our discussion of the survey method. The process can be illustrated in a variety of ways; but one which is especially revealing is the changing imagery which social scientists have used to describe their own role over the years. August Comte, the Frenchman who first coined the word 'sociology' in 1825 or so, tended to describe the role of the social scientist – to our eyes extravagantly – as philosopher-kings or priests. He saw social science and social scientists as the central quasi-religious authority in the newly emergent industrial order, and, perhaps naturally, drew a parallel between this authority and the old of the monarchy and church. However, the twentieth century saw the development of a view of the social scientist as professional; as in the work of Emile Durkheim, writing in France at the turn of the present century. For Durkheim the relevant imagery had changed from that of the social scientist as authority figure with the power to change social arrangements, to that of an independent expert having specialised knowledge.[2] It is interesting to note that although Durkheim was a professor working within the French state educational system, a system which he did much to develop and promote, he chose to emphasise the elements of independence so important to the rhetoric of professionals everywhere.

The idea of independent professionalism has been an important and recurring motif in the development of social sciences, but nowhere more so than in America. In Britain we have observed that the substantial incorporation of social science into the bureaucratic structures of the capitalist state was achieved relatively early, and only subsequently with that process fully accomplished have social scientists sought to emphasise the supposed independence required by professional status. In the USA, the process worked the other way around, with the emphasis on professionalism preceding the full incorporation of social science into a bureaucratic political and economic order.

Whatever the precise process, however, the impulse towards professionalisation can be seen at all times as an important motivation for social scientists, and where significant headway has been made in successfully achieving a monopoly on some definite area of knowledge, the incorporation of social science into bureaucratic structures, whether they be economic or administrative, has been facilitated. However, it is the development of claims to esoteric knowledge which is the *sine qua non* of professionalisation, in which research expertise is a central ingredient. It is this knowledge which underwrites their claim to professional status, and it is their professional status which makes them the products of their social circumstances, and gives their knowledge a particular role within society.

From Comte onwards the impulse for social change and reform has driven sociologists, and many other social scientists, onward, seeking through their knowledge for ways of improving or at least ameliorating the lot of their fellow men. Unlike most practising politicians, investigative journalists, Utopians, and 'do-gooders', they generally sought to base their reforming zeal on good, sound scientific knowledge of society and how it works. Both Durkheim and Weber shared, in different ways, this desire to understand the social forces which shaped men's fate so that they could be better controlled and used for a greater benefit. Marx, too, though revolutionary rather than reformist in his aspirations, similarly sought to develop a scientific method to explain and evaluate societies. However, with the institutional-isation and professionalisation of social science, far greater emphasis was placed on the *science* aspect than on the practical or the applied. Even Weber, who was frequently involved in live political issues in Germany, stressed the importance of value neutrality on the part of the social scientist *qua* scientist, and so we begin to see the slow, gradual, and often unclear distinction between social science and practical, directed social change.

Some of this pattern we have detected in our discussion of methods of data collection. Booth and Rowntree, for example, were motivated by deeply felt concerns about the dreadful conditions under which a large proportion of their fellow countrymen lived. The facts they provided played a considerable part in the growth of the welfare state in this country. Their aims were the relatively modest ones of providing facts about a clearly stated problem so that others might be persuaded to do something about it. They were little interested in theory as understood today, and did not provide much of a model for the professional social scientist who is master of an esoteric body of knowledge. In this respect the early symbolic interactionists in Chicago might have established a more viable role model. They were learned enough in the philosophy and social science of their time, had a strong and definite point of view, and a number of them committed to change and reform. They also had a method, namely, participant observation. Acquiring competence and the craft of sociological research was a long and arduous apprenticeship but, as we have seen, this did not result in the kind of codified and propositional knowledge which could form the basis of engineered reform. On the contrary, many symbolic interactionists were to argue that such knowledge of society was difficult, if not impossible, to achieve. Society, social life, could only be revealed and preserved like the specimens in a museum.

There were, however, other attempts, especially in the United States in the 1920s and 1930s, practically to apply scientific ideas to social organisation. Sociologists, psychologists, and anthropologists interested particularly in industrial organisations began to undertake research on a consultancy basis with the aim of engineering changes within such organisations. Some extravagant claims were made about the actual or potential efficacy of such practical intervention. Elton Mayo, a founding father of industrial sociology, suggested, for example, that if social scientific knowledge had kept pace with material technology then major social disaster, such as war, could be prevented.[3]

Whether such claims are in any way defensible is not a matter that can really detain us here. But it is worth noting that the practical value of social scientific knowledge which was emphasised by many scholars at that time in the USA did not receive a sympathetic hearing for long, nor has it recurred with such naïve vigour since.[4] These days the methodological injunction to the researcher not to influence the subjects he or she studies is emphasised, whatever the methodological device or technique involved. Even the small achievements of those scholars who did advocate active attempts to bring about change has been rewritten so as to reflect this dominant view. An example may help to illustrate these points. For Elton Mayo co-operation was a key idea. He saw social science as attempting to gain practical knowledge of social life, and there seems little doubt that these ideas strongly influenced the early stages of a famous research programme carried out in Chicago at the time. The early phases of this research, now popularly known as the Hawthorne study, were primarily concerned with discovering the administrative circumstances under which co-operation could best be fostered, with the aim of using this knowledge to raise the level of satisfaction workers gain from work and, consequently, productivity. In the interval between the conduct of the research and its publication (approximately the period 1929–39) the idea that co-operation was fostered and that improvements in worker satisfaction and responsiveness was a socially engineered outcome was completely obscured. The early phases of the Hawthorne research were reinterpreted as objective experiments in which the participants were exposed to a series of different stimuli, and the capacity of research workers actually to foster co-operation was now taken to be a most unfortunate 'accidental' effect. In most methods texts the label 'Hawthorne effect' is used to designate instances where the researcher might accidentally affect the outcome of his research by his participation. That this can happen easily enough is used as a warning, and to take care not to influence the human beings encountered in research. In short, to stress the importance of maintaining a rigid 'neutrality' in all research dealings with subjects.[5]

No doubt special circumstances, such as economic recessions and crisis, the emergence of Fascism in Europe, and the threat of war, contributed to the short-lived popularity of the practical value of social science. Whatever the reason, it soon receded. Both radicals and conservatives criticised those who attempted to develop practical but restricted applications of social scientific knowledge. The charge was made, for example, that far from introducing any reforms, the real effect of organisational change consequent on the application of social science was simply to adapt the people in them more fully to the interests of those controlling them. Or, alternatively, it was held that practical involvements interfere with the supposed ethical neutrality of science: an important sentiment to the professional social scientist.

Although the symbolic interactionists remained as a viable professional role model for the social scientist, its influence did not stay dominant for long. In the 1920s and 1930s it was simply the most fully articulated viewpoint in sociology, and susceptible of supporting the research activities of a number of variants of social behaviourism. As we have seen, social behaviourism was dramatically overtaken by sociological functionalism as the dominant theoretical orthodoxy in the United States and to an important extent also in the rest of the sociological Western world. Once again, however, the impulse toward professionalism was formative in this development, and once again research methods were the road upon which the claim to esoteric knowledge could be successfully advanced. Hence, hand in hand with the emergence to prominence of sociological functionalism, we have the substantial development of the survey and statistical methods in social science. Soon, within the sociological establishment, the dominant orthodoxy of functionalist theory and statistically analysed survey methods had little to challenge them. There were important areas of residual loyalty to symbolic interactionism with its apparently more humane and liberal view of human behaviour and human agency, but its unsystematic – indeed unsystematisable – methods of data collection and analysis seemed hopelessly amateur by comparison. Survey methods had, in their use of computers to analyse results statistically, the merit of making use of modern technology, and so made a direct appeal to the imagery of modern science and technology as the basis of the social scientist's claims to professional expertise.

In recent years, however, the professional model has come under criticism from a number of directions. In Britain and Europe, for example, there has been a renewed interest in the Marxist social scientific tradition with its emphasis on developing a critical theoretical posture directed against the institutions of contemporary capitalism. Such a tradition fits uneasily with the idea of the social scientist as professional. Methodologically speaking, however, since the mid-1960s growing concern has been expressed in a number of quarters about the very bases of social scientific knowledge, and the intellectual warrants upon which methods of social research were held to rest. There has been a tendency for some social scientists at least to become more sophisticated, and perhaps more cynical, in their assessment of the empiricist tradition which has largely supported the development of methods of research. There is now a more widespread recognition that 'facts' are not so much ineluctible features of reality as productions significant only within a given context of meaning.

Not surprisingly, there are a number of versions of this criticism of the empiricism which has largely dominated the development of research methods. However, most of them arise out of much the same feeling of disquiet over the alleged failure of the social sciences to emulate successfully the achievements of the natural sciences. Despite an apparently impressive technology of methods of data collection and analysis there seems little to show in the way of powerfully wrought theories, the precise measurement of social variables, or knowledge which could prove, in some sense, useful. Some diagnose this state of affairs as due to the inevitable infusion of values into social research, while others see it mainly in terms of the immaturity of the social sciences. But, whatever the diagnosis, what is relatively clear is the growing lack of confidence in empirical research methods.

One way of looking at this matter is in terms of the methods of data collection we have discussed in this book: the survey and interview, and participant observation. We have argued that no methods can be considered as neutral atheoretical tools since they embody theories, often implicitly, about the nature of the social actor and the relationships he or she has with others. Many of these implicit theories, the 'instrumental presuppositions' as we called them in Chapter 1, are profoundly social in their reference. Even the apparently non-sociological theories of random sampling, as we have seen, imply something about the way in which the sampling units, usually individuals, are related. They embody or have relevance for, in short, theories of social relationships. And, as we pointed out, the methodological issue is whether or not such theories are consistent with the wider theoretical presuppositions of the discipline which uses them. Of course, this particular methodological problem is compounded when we examine the rationale behind each of the methods discussed. What is clear, for example, is that the survey method is predicated on a rather different image of society and the social actor to that of participant observation. One could say, in brief, that each produce different data: data that only have meaning within the method which produces them. If this is correct, it means that we cannot, in principle, compare the data produced by different methods, nor, further, effectively choose between the theories the data are claimed to support.

One response to the general disquiet is to search for even more refined techniques of data collection and, more especially, data analysis, though it would probably be incorrect to see this purely as a response to the present situation since it has been a growing tendency since the 1930s, and has merely been given added impetus by the appraisal now being brought to bear on the methods of social science.[6] However, such a response fails to avoid the view we have criticised in these pages which sees methods as highly elaborate technological practices. It consists merely in a recapitulation of the 'nature of the problem' and the 'nature of the instrument' models of research methods, failing to recognise that research problems follow from what are theoretical issues and which we ignore at the cost of misunderstanding what it is we are doing.

A rather more promising response to the general problem of

inter-method and inter-data comparability is the notion of triangulation with respect to data, method, and theory.[7] The argument has the virtue of at least recognising that within the social sciences 'empirical reality is a reality of competing definitions, attitudes and personal values' and research has no option but to recognise this fully and reach beyond the biases that arise from single methodologies, Denzin recommends four basic types of triangulation: data with respect to time, place, person, and level of analysis; investigation in terms of multiple versus single observers of the same phenomenon; theory by using single perspectives in relation to the same set of phenomena; and last, but not least, methodological, involving comparisons both within and between method. The strategy involves using, for example, as many data sources as possible to illuminate the same object-matter, using different methods, a variety of measures, different observers, and so forth, so that by 'combining multiple observers, theories, methods and data sources sociologists can hope to overcome the intrinsic bias that comes from single-method, single-observer, single-theory studies'.[8]

Though there are obvious practical difficulties in implementing such a programme as Denzin recommends, the strategy, on the face of it at least, has much to commend it. But, it cannot avoid consideration of the sort of issues we have been raising so far though, practically speaking, a research project established on these lines might serve as a forcing house where these issues are likely to come to the fore rather more quickly than they might have done.

Another and perhaps more direct and insightful response to the problems we have identified is provided by Cicourel and others who, in the mid-1960s, began to mount a criticism of social science research methods from the 'inside', as it were.[9] They took very seriously indeed the contention that social research is a social act and not some aseptic circumstance of the sort presumed, or at least desired, by many investigators.[10] Cicourel himself criticises orthodox research methods for failing to develop theories of data which incorporate rather than gloss the actor's subjective viewpoint and the meanings he, or she, uses to make sense of and create social reality. As we have seen in the case of the interview, the rules of research practice seem to have a considerable part to play in constructing a version of the actor's social reality at the expense of a serious examination of how, in fact, meanings and actions are accomplished by actors. The research act, as we have stressed, is a *social* act and many of the theories of instrumentation which underpin research methods are accordingly substantive sociological theories in their own right. So, among the alternative explanations which may be consistent with a set of data, will be theories which have to do with the way the data are generated as part of the research process itself. What is clear from Cicourel's perspective is that the participants in the research encounter, both investigator and subject, make use of implicit, common-sense knowledge, or theories about the social worlds in which they live, to create what turns out as data. The point is that little of this is ever an explicit part of the instrumental or theoretical presuppositions of the method.

Unlike the strategy of triangulation, this critique is derived from an explicit conception of the actor and society which is deemed to have consequences for the methods and the general character of social research. It is a view which argues that social reality does not exist in any objective or external way, as Durkheim held, independently of the work and resources social actors use to construct it. Social reality is created and sustained by the members of society through the language and the meanings they use. On this view, social reality becomes an 'intersubjective' phenomenon and an ongoing accomplishment of members, not some disembodied assemblage of structures and forces.

As we have indicated, this critique follows from particular conceptions of the social actor and social life and amounts to a very serious attack on most of the orthodox methods of social research. Many of the criticisms we have earlier voiced about the interview and questionnaire, for example, derive in large part from this body of thought. Quite what it recommends as a method for studying social life is another matter. In his earlier work Cicourel himself does not wish to write off social *science* as being, in principle, impossible, merely that it has failed to develop adequate theories of instrumentation. Others, such as some ethnomethodologists, have devoted their efforts to elucidating the sense assembly procedures used by members, especially in their talk, to accomplish social sense.[11] In any event, a less than sharp distinction, to go back to points made earlier in this chapter, is made between professionalised sociological knowledge and that possessed by members. They charge professional sociology with reducing, unwittingly perhaps, the social actor to a 'judgemental dope' rather than perceiving him, or her, as endowed with the ability to use and develop the social theories necessary for competent social performance. The social scientist becomes more of a collaborator with subjects than a detached professional possessing esoteric scientific knowledge. Of necessity, perhaps, the view places less emphasis on formalised methodology and places its stress instead on observation, including participant observation, of naturally occurring social productions.[12]

Ultimately, of course, these criticisms reach up to major issues in the philosophy of social science. However, from the point of view of the practice of social research we can say that there is currently a movement to rethink both its methods and its justifications. As always, opinions do differ on what line to take, as we have just seen, but one matter is of recurrent concern and interest; a focus of interest we might generally term, 'the social context of method'. Broadly speaking, we can identify three perspectives on this. First, it involves the recognition that much of data collection in social science takes place in a social context. That is, much of the actual business of research involves social encounters which can be studied in their own right. Second, social research is produced by groups, and here interest focuses on the relationships between them, the source of their ideas, how they come to be modified or developed, and so forth.[13] Third, and finally, there is the fact that social science takes place within a particular society at a given point in history. This is the broadest sense in which social science can be said to have a social context. The development of society as a whole is the context in which social science itself changes, and these processes are likely to shape the concerns and interests of social scientists themselves.

In the course of this book we have, if rather unsystematically and unevenly, raised issues to do with many of these themes.

We have tried to demonstrate with regard to particular methods of data collection that they are not merely tools devised to meet particular ends, but expedients which have meaning only when considered in their social context defined in the broadest sense considered here. Yet for all our argument that the methods of data collection are in a very general sense social events, we do not see them as being fundamentally compromised because of this.

No science can entirely escape its social context. In the case of social science it is questionable whether this is either necessary or desirable. However, reviewing the methods of data collection we have discussed in this book in a general way, it is evident that the professionalisation of social science and its incorporation into the institutional structure of societies such as our own has had some unhappy consequences. We have argued that, among other things, this leads to a generally passive attitude towards the subjects of social science. People are seen merely as sources of data. But manifestly they are more than this. They are also active and receptive agents capable of independent action, which social science can either facilitate or obstruct.

Perhaps the most serious consequence of the devaluation or ignoring of the social context of method is that it also involves a devaluation of the social nature of man. No method of data collection need be merely a method of data collection. Failure to recognise the human capacity for independent and autonomous action is, dare we suggest, also a moral and political failure.

REFERENCES AND FURTHER READING

Chapter 1 Data and research practice

1. There is, of course much ongoing debate about the nature of social science and, especially, the relationship between theory and the empirical world. A full discussion of these matters is beyond the scope of this book. But, for example, A. Ryan, *The Philosophy of the Social Sciences*, London, Macmillan, 1970; A. Kaplan, *The Conduct of Inquiry*, San Francisco, Chandler, 1964; P. Diesing, *Patterns of Discovery in the Social Sciences*, London, Routledge and Kegan Paul, 1972, are more than useful.
2. See for general discussion on this issue, John A. Hughes, *The Philosophy of Social Research*, London, Longman, 1980.
3. D. Willer and J. Willer, *Systematic Empiricism: A Critique of Pseudo-Science*, Englewood Cliffs, Prentice-Hall, 1974.
4. G. Easthope, *A History of Social Research Methods*, London, Longman, 1974, Ch. 3. Of course, procedures similar to the modern survey have been used since ancient times. What makes the modern social survey different from its ancient predecessors are the theories which underwrite its use. See Chapter 3 of this book.
5. E. Durkheim, *Suicide*, London, Routledge and Kegan Paul, 1952.
6. H. Blumer, *Symbolic Interaction*, Englewood Cliffs, Prentice-Hall, 1969, p. 53. See also the excellent book by P. Rock, *The Making of Symbolic Interactionism*, London, Macmillan, 1979.
7. N. K. Denzin, *The Research Act*, Chicago, Aldine, 1970, p. 298. Also John A. Hughes, *Sociological Analysis: Methods of Discovery*, London, Nelson, 1976.
8. C. Taylor, 'Interpretation and the sciences of man' in R. Bechler and A. R. Drengson (eds), *The Philosophy of Society*, London, Methuen, 1978, pp. 156–200.
9. A. V. Cicourel, *Method and Measurement in Sociology*, New York, The Free Press, 1965; H. Mehan and H. Wood, *The Reality of Ethnomethodology*, New York, Wiley, 1975.
10. See Rock, op. cit.

Chapter 2   Data and social theory

1. For treatment of the philosophy of social science see, for example, A. Ryan, *The Philosophy of Social Science*, London, Macmillan, 1970; R. S. Rudner, *Philosophy of Social Science*, Englewood Cliffs, Prentice-Hall, 1966; M. Lessnoff, *The Structure of Social Science*, London, Allen and Unwin, 1974; D. Popineau, *For Science in the Social Sciences*, London, Macmillan, 1978; J. A. Hughes, *The Philosophy of Social Research*, London, Longman, 1980; R. Keat and J. Urry, *Social Theory as Science*, London, Routledge and Kegan Paul, 1975.

2. See Hughes, op. cit.; T. Benton, *Philosophical Foundations of the Three Sociologies*, London, Routledge and Kegan Paul, 1977.

3. See J. S. Mill, *A System of Logic*, London, Longman, 1965 edn.

4. See R. Brown, *Rules and Laws in Sociology*, London, Routledge and Kegan Paul, 1973, for an excellent discussion of generalisations in social science.

5. This model owes much to the work of K. Popper, *The Logic of Scientific Discovery*, London, Hutchinson, 1959; J. O, Wisdom, *Foundations of Inference in Natural Science*, London, Methuen, 1952; A. Stinchcombe, *Constructing Social Theories*, New York, Harcourt, Brace and World, 1968.

6. See Stinchcombe, op. cit., p. 22. Also, D. T. Campbell, 'Prospective: artifact and control' in R. Rosenthal and R. L. Rosnow (eds), *Artifact in Behavioural Research*, New York, Academic Press, 1969.

7. See, for example, R. Bashar, *A Realist Theory of Science*, London, Harvester Press, 1978; R. Keat and J. Urry, *Social Theory as Science*, London, Routledge and Kegan Paul, 1975; D. Willer and J. Willer, *Systematic Empiricism*, Englewood Cliffs, Prentice-Hall, 1973.

8. T. Kuhn, *The Structure of Scientific Revolutions*, 2nd edn, Chicago, University of Chicago Press, 1970.

9. On Durkheim, see his *Rules of Sociological Method*, Glencoe, The Free Press, 1966, G. E. C. Catlin (ed.).

10. The authoritative tradition for this concept is a long one, of course, see, for example, R. A. Nisbet, *The Sociological Tradition*, London, Heinemann, 1967, Ch. 7, for a discussion of the concept of alienation and its historical roots. Also, M. Seeman, 'On the meaning of alienation', *American Sociological Review*, 24, 1959.

11. E. Durkheim *Suicide*, London, Routledge and Kegan Paul, 1952.

12. See, for example, J. M. Atkinson, *Discovering Suicide*, London, Macmillan, 1978, for a discussion of these themes.

13. But see B. Hindess, *The Use of Official Statistics in Sociology*, London, Macmillan, 1973.

14. This approach has survived a remarkably long time. See for example, E. A. Johns, *The Social Structure of Modern Britain*, Harmondsworth, Penguin, 1965.

15. This notion owes much to the work of P. F. Lazarsfeld. See, for example, his 'A conceptual introduction to latent structure analysis' in P. F. Lazarsfeld (ed), *Mathematical Thinking in the Social Sciences*, Glencoe, The Free Press, 1954. All the work on attitude scaling belongs to this conception.

16. M. Hesse, 'Theory and value in the social sciences' in C. Hookway and P. Peltit (eds), *Action and Interpretation*, Cambridge, Cambridge University Press, 1978, pp.1–16.

17. This position leads on to a consideration of the hermeneutic tradition in social science. See, for example, C. Taylor, 'Interpretation and the sciences

of man' in R. Beehler and A. R. Drengson (eds), *The Philosophy of Society*, London, Methuen, 1978, pp. 156–200.

18. See for a critique of this, J. Coulter, 'Beliefs and practical understanding' in G. Psathas (ed), *Everyday Language*, New York, Wiley, 1979, pp. 163–86.

19. See Hughes, op. cit., for a discussion of alternatives to this orthodox view of the elements we have just discussed. Also, T. P. Wilson, 'Normative and interpretive paradigms in sociology' in J. Douglas (ed.), *Understanding Everyday Life*, London Routledge and Kegan Paul, 1971, pp. 57–79.

Chapter 3 Social surveys

1. See, for example, T. S. and M. B. Simey, *Charles Booth, Social Scientist*, London, Oxford University Press, 1960; A. Briggs, 'B. Seebohm Rowntree 1871–1954' in A. Briggs and J. Saville (eds), *Essays in Labour History*, London, Macmillan, 2 vols, 1960 and 1971; C. Booth (ed.), *Life and Labour of the People of London*, London, Macmillan, 1892–97; B. S. Rowntree, *Poverty: A Study in Town Life*, London, Macmillan, 1901.

2. Booth, in particular, conducted studies of the census data before he began his own more detailed investigations. See 'Occupations of the People of the United Kingdom 1801–1881', *Journal of the Royal Statistical Society*, June 1886. For some comments on Booth's life and contribution to social science see G. Easthope, *A History of Social Research Methods*, London, Longman, 1974, pp. 49–55.

3. D. V. Glass, *Numbering the People : The Eighteenth Century Population Controversy*, London, Gordon and Clemonisi, 1973.

4. B. Hindess, *The Uses of Official Statistics in Sociology*, London, Macmillan, 1973. See also Glass, op. cit.

5. R. G. D. Allen in *A Dictionary of National Biography 1959–1961*, London, Oxford University Press, 1971.

6. The term is taken from G. H. Sabine, *A History of Political Theory*, London, Harrap, 1960 (3rd edn). For an interesting commentary on the relationship between sociology and liberalism, see S. Collini, *Sociology and Liberalism*, London, Cambridge University Press, 1979.

7. See M. Abrams, *Social Surveys and Social Action*, London, Heinemann, 1951, Ch. 10.

8. C. A. Moser, *Survey Methods in Social Investigation*, London, Heinemann, 1958 (1st edn), p. 23.

9. Ibid., p. 25.

10. D. MacKenzie, 'Eugenics and the rise of mathematical statistics in Britain'; and M. Shaw and I. Miles, 'The social roots of social knowledge' in J. L. Irvine et al. (eds), *Demystifying Social Statistics*, London, Pluto Press, 1979.

11. See, for example, F. Conway, *Sampling*, London, George Allen and Unwin, 1967; F. Yates, *Sampling Methods for Censuses and Surveys*, London, Griffin (3rd edn.), 1960.

12. For further details see, for example, C. A Moser and G. Kalton, *Survey Methods in Social Investigation*, London, Heinemann (2nd edn.), 1971, pp. 85–116.

13. See A. L Bowley and A. R. Burnett-Hurst, *Livelihood and Poverty*, London, G. Bell, 1915; A. L. Bowley and M. H. Hogg, *Has Poverty Diminished?*, London, P. S. King, 1925.

14. Quoted by G. Gallup and S. F. Rae, *The Pulse of Democracy*, New York, Simon and Schuster, 1940, p. 6.

15. Abrams, op. cit., pp. 53–62.

16. For a summary account of the US Straw Poll see J. Madge, *The Tools of Social Science*, London, Longman, 1953. Citing C. E. Robinson, Madge suggests that there may have been some manipulation of the results in order to influence the outcome of the election. Abrams, op. cit., also offers some perceptive remarks on the Straw Poll, see especially pp. 64–5.

17. See for example, Moser and Kalton, op. cit., pp. 127–37; Madge, *Tools of Social Science*, pp. 212–13.

18. See T. H. Marshall, 'A British sociological career', *British Journal of Sociology*, 24, No. 4, 399–408.

19. L. L. and J. Barnard, *Origins of American Sociology*, New York, Crowell, 1943; J. Madge, *Origins of Scientific Sociology*, London, Tavistock, 1963, especially Ch. 1; K. H. Wolf, 'Notes towards a socio-cultural interpretation of American sociology', *American Sociological Review*, 11, 1946, 545–53.

20. J. D. Y. Peel, *Herbert Spencer: The Evolution of a Sociologist*, London, Heinemann, 1971, p. 249.

21. D. Martindale, *The Nature and Types of Sociological Theory*, London, Routledge and Kegan Paul, 1960, p. 520. See also L. Bramson, *The Political Context of Sociology*, Princeton, Princeton University Press, 1961.

22. Writing in 1959, C. Wright Mills suggests that American sociology is monopolised by 'grand theory', which was predominantly functionalist; and 'abstracted empiricism' which was predominantly statistical. C. Wright Mills, *The Sociological Imagination*, New York, Oxford University Press, 1959.

23. See, for example, R. E. L. Faris, *Chicago Sociology, 1920–32*, Chicago, University of Chicago Press, 1967; P. Rock, *The Making of Symbolic Interactionism*, London, Macmillan, 1979; A. Carey, *Sociology and Public Affairs*, New York, Sage, 1978.

24. W. I. Thomas and F. Znanieki, *The Polish Peasant in Europe and America*, New York, Knopf, 1927; also for an account of this research, see Madge, *Origins of Scientific Sociology*, Ch. 3.

25. R. S. and H. M. Lynd, *Middletown: A Study in Contemporary Culture*, New York, Harcourt Brace, 1929. See also Madge, *Origins of Scientific Sociology* Ch. 5.

26. J. Brown and B. G. Gilmartin, 'Sociology today: lacunae, emphases, surfeits', *American Sociologist*, 4, 1968. See also D. L. Phillips, *Knowledge From What?* New York, Rand McNally, 1971, Ch. 1.

27. See, for example, Martindale, op. cit.

28. T. W. Adorno et al., *The Authoritarian Personality*, New York, Harper, 1950.

29. See R. Christie and M. Jahoda, *Continuities in Social Research*, New York, Free Press, 1954, p. 120.

30. P. F. Lazarsfeld et al., *The People's Choice*, New York, Columbia University Press, 1944.

31. For an account of panel and other types of longitudinal studies see W. D Wall and H. L. Williams, *Longitudinal Studies and the Social Sciences*, Heinemann, London, 1970.

32. See R. A. Fisher, *The Design of Experiments*. Edinburgh, Oliver and Boyd, 1937.

33. J. A. Hughes, *Sociological Analysis*, London, Nelson, 1976, pp. 86–8. See

also S. Stouffer, 'Some observations on study design', *American Journal of Sociology*, 53, 1950, 355–61; D. T. Campbell and J. C. Stanley, *Experimental and Quasi Experimental Designs For Research*, Chicago, Rand McNally, 1963; J. L. Myers, *Fundamentals of Experimental Design*, New York, Allyn and Bacon (2nd edn.), 1972.

34. See P. F Lazarsfeld and M. Rosenberg (eds), *The Language of Social Research*, New York, Free Press, 1955, pp. 40–53; H. H. Hyman, *Survey Design and Analysis*, New York, Free Press, 1955; A. N. Oppenheim, *Questionnaire Design and Attitude Measurement*, London, Heinemann, 1966; J. A. Davis, *Elementary Survey Analysis*, Englewood Cliffs, Prentice-Hall, 1971.

35. See R. E. Henkel and D. E. Morrison (eds), *The Significance Test Controversy*, London, Butterworths, 1970; L. Atkins and D. Jarrett, 'The significance of "Significance Tests"' in Irvine et al., op. cit.

36. E. Powers 'An experiment in the prevention of delinquency', selections reprinted in M. W. Riley, *Sociological Research: A Case Approach*, New York, Harcourt Brace, 1963, pp. 572–80.

37. See E. G. Boring, 'Perspective: artifact and control' in R. Rosenthal and R. L. Rosnow (eds), *Artifact in Behavioural Research*, New York, Academic Press, 1969. See also, N. J. Friedman, *The Social Nature of Psychological Research*, New York, Basic Books, 1967.

38. J. Galtung, *Theory and Methods of Social Research*, London, Allen and Unwin, 1967, p. 150.

39. Ibid., p. 151.

Chapter 4 Interviewing

1. See M. Benney and E. C. Hughes, 'Of sociology and the interview', *American Journal of Sociology*, 62, 1956, 137–42; J. Brown and G. Gilmartin, 'Sociology today: lacunae, emphases and surfeits', *American Sociologist*, 4, 1969, 283–91, report that 91 per cent of the research articles published in two major American sociology journals had gathered data by means of the interview and or questionnaire.

2. A. L. Bowley, *Elements of Statistics*, London, Curtis (3rd edn.), 1937, pp. 20–1. Also quoted by J. Madge, *The Tools of Social Science*, London, Longman, 1953, p. 179.

3. R. K. Merton et al., *The Focussed Interview*, New York, Free Press, 1951.

4. See A. N. Oppenheim, *Questionnaire Design and Attitude Measurement*, London, Heinemann, 1966; W. J. Goode and P. K. Hatt, *Methods in Social Research*, New York, McGraw-Hill, 1952.

5. A. Orenstein and W. F. R. Phillips, *Understanding Social Research*, Boston, Allyn and Bacon, 1978, p. 222.

6. If 'don't know' or 'no answer' responses constitute a large proportion of the replies, this is normally taken as an indication that the range of alternatives provided by the question are failing to tap the range of relevant responses.

7. J. Madge, *Origins of Scientific Sociology*, London, Tavistock, 1963, p. 532.

8. Benney and Hughes, op. cit.

9. Ibid.

10. See J. M. Converse and H. Schuman, *Conversations at Random*, New York, Wiley, 1974.

11. H. H. Hyman et al. *Interviewing in Social Research*, Chicago, University of Chicago Press, 1954, pp. 238–40.

12. A. L. Edwards, 'The relationship between the judged desirability of a trait and the probability that the trait will be endorsed', *Journal of Applied Psychology*, **37**, 1953, 90–3. Also, D. Crowne and D. Marlow, *The Approval Motive*, New York, Wiley , 1964.

13. B. Dohrenwend, 'Social status and psychological disorder: an issue of substance and an issue of method', *American Sociological Review*, **31**, 1966, 14–34; D. L. Phillips, *Knowledge From What?* Chicago, Rand McNally, 1971, pp. 39–47, contains a summary of many such studies. See also his *Abandoning Method*, San Francisco, Jossey-Bass, 1973, Chs 2 and 3.

14. See, for example, C. G. Ball and W. Buchanan, 'Reliable and unreliable respondents: party registration and prestige pressure', *Western Political Quarterly*, **29**, 1966, 37–43. D. Cahalan, 'Correlates of response accuracy in the Denver validity study', *Public Opinion Quarterly*, **32**, 1968, 607–21.

15. Hyman et al. put the problem this way: 'Whether or not interviewers differ in the results they obtain, there is also the problem of whether any or all of them obtain accurate results, results that approximate some true values.' Op. cit., p. 20.

16. See, for example, Hyman, et al., ibid., and R. Kahn and C. F. Cannell, *The Dynamics of Interviewing*, New York, Wiley, 1957.

17. See A. V. Cicourel, *Method and Measurement in Sociology*, New York, Free Press, 1964, for an extensive critique of the interview.

18. A. C. Kinsey et al., *Sexual Behaviour in the Human Male*, Philadelphia, Saunders, 1948. For a commentary on this study see Madge, *Origins of Scientific Sociology*, Ch. 10. The technique illustrates the point being made here in that since Kinsey's study was dealing with the sensitive topic of sexual behaviour in the 1940s, about which people were reluctant to talk, methods encouraging respondents to be more open were necessary.

19. I. Deutscher, 'Asking questions cross-culturally: some problems of Linguistic comparability', in H. S. Becker et al. (eds), *Institutions and the Person*, Chicago, Aldine, 1968, pp.318–41.

20. See, for example, K. R. Athey, 'Two experiments showing the effects of the interviewer's racial background in response to questionnaires concerning racial issues', *Journal of Applied Psychology*, **44**, 1960, 244–6; M. Benney, D. Riesman, and S. A. Star, 'Age and sex in the interview', *American Journal of Sociology* , **62**, 1956, 143–52; Hyman, et al, op. cit.; Kahn and Cannell, op. cit.

21. H. Schuman and J. Converse, 'The effects of black and white interviewers on black responses in 1968', *Public Opinion Quarterly*, **35**, 1971, 44–68. Also reported in Orenstein and Phillips, op. cit., p. 233.

22. See, for example, D. Katz, 'Do interviews bias poll results?', *Public Opinion Quarterly*, **6**, 1942, 248–68; B. S. Dohrenwend et al., 'Social distance and interviewer effects', *Public Opinion Quarterly*, **32**, 1968, 410–22; Orenstein and Phillips, op. cit., pp. 234–5.

23. C. Wright Mills, 'Language, logic and culture' in I. Horowitz (ed.), *Power, Politics and People*, Oxford University Press, New York, 1963, p. 433. See also R. F. Mitchell, 'Survey materials collected in developing countries: sampling, measurement and interviewing obstacles', *International Social Science Journal*, **17**, 1965; E. Scheuch, 'The cross-cultural use of sample surveys: problems of comparability' in R. Rokkan (ed.), *Comparative Research Across Cultures and Nations*, Paris, Mouton, 1968.

24. Deutscher, op. cit.
25. Of course, pollsters tend to interview a number of times prior to an election, which gives an indication of movement of voting behaviour and intentions.
26. Deutscher, op. cit.
27. See J. Heritage, 'Assessing people' in J. Armistead (ed.), *Reconstructing Social Psychology*, Harmondsworth, Penguin, 1965.
28. This, of course, was realised by proponents of survey method; see Hyman, op. cit., p. 30.
29. A. V. Cicourel, *Theory and Method in the Study of Argentine Fertility*, New York, Wiley, 1974, is an excellent study of interviewing methods.
30. J. Galtung, *Theory and Methods in Social Research*, London, George Allen and Unwin, 1972, Ch. 6.
31. Converse and Schuman, op. cit., p. 94.
32. H. Mehan and H. Wood, *The Reality of Ethnomethodology*, New York, Wiley, 1975, p. 49.
33. Ibid., p. 49.
34. Cicourel, op. cit., and also his *Method and Measurement in Sociology*, New York, Free Press, 1964.
35. Cicourel, *Method and Measurement in Sociology* , pp. 100–4.
36. Ibid., p. 51.

Chapter 5 Participant observation

1. The study of members' methods of negotiating everyday life is the focus of the recently developed ethnomethodology. See, for example, J. Douglas, *Understanding Everyday Life*, London, Routledge and Kegan Paul, 1971; H. Mehan and H. Wood, *The Reality of Ethnomethodology*, New York, Wiley, 1965.
2. H. S. Becker and B. Geer, 'Participant observation and interviewing: a comparison' in W. J. Filstead (ed.), *Qualitative Methodology*, Chicago, Markham, 1970, p. 133. This volume contains much valuable information on participant observation.
3. It has often been noted that even the briefest of contacts between investigator and subject can have a measurable effect on the way the subjects perceive the test situation. See, for example, R. Rosenthal, *Experimenter Effects in Behavioural Research*, New York, Appleton-Century-Crofts, 1966.
4. T. S. and M. B. Simey, *Charles Booth: Social Scientist*, New York, Oxford University Press, 1960. See also, G. Easthope, *A History of Social Research Methods*, London, Longman, 1974, p. 59.
5. As, for example, in the encyclopaedic work of Sir James Frazer, whose *Golden Bough* was first published in 1890 and extended to 12 volumes of collected reportage by 1915. See J. G. Frazer, *The Golden Bough*, London, Macmillan (abridged edn.), 1957.
6. B. Malinowski, *Argonauts of the Western Pacific*, London, Routledge and Kegan Paul, 1922.
7. Jason Ditton's, *Part-time Crime*, London, Macmillan, 1977, is an ethnographic study of bakery workers and delivery men. There have been many studies of industrial workers using this method. Few eclipse the work of D. F. Roy. See, for example, his 'Quota restriction and gold-bricking in a machine shop', *American Journal of Sociology*, 57, 1952.

8. See A. L. Epstein, *The Craft of Social Anthropology*, London, Tavistock, 1967.
9. See R. E. L. Faris, *Chicago Sociology: 1920–32*, Chicago, University of Chicago Press, 1967.
10. Many texts competently outline the contribution of these men. See, for example, D. Martindale, *Nature and Types of Sociological Theory*, London, Routledge and Kegan Paul, 1961; H. E. Barnes (ed.), *Introduction to the History of Sociology*, Chicago, University of Chicago Press, 1948; H. P. Becker and H. E. Barnes, *Social Thought From Lore to Science, Vol. 2.*, New York, Dover, 1952.
11. Becker and Barnes, op. cit.; L. Bramson, *The Political Context of Sociology*, Princeton, Princeton University Press, 1961.
12. W. G. Summer's most celebrated work is his *Folkways*, New York, Mentor Books, 1960. For an informative discussion of the influence of Spencer on Sumner, see H. E. Barnes 'W. G. Sumner: Spencerianism in American Press' in Barnes, op. cit.
13. C. W. Mills, 'The professional ideology of the social pathologists', *American Journal of Sociology*, **49**, 1943.
14. P. Rock. *The Making of Symbolic Interactionism*, London, Macmillan, 1979, p. 92. This is an excellent study of the development of the theory of interactionism and the place of participant observation.
15. Ibid., p. 92.
16. N. Anderson, *The Hobo*, Chicago, University of Chicago Press (2nd edn), 1961. F. M. Thrasher, *The Gang*, Chicago, University of Chicago Press, 1963: P. G. Cressey, *The Taxi Dance Hall*, Chicago, University of Chicago Press, 1932. See also Faris, op. cit.
17. E. C. Lindeman, *Social Discovery*, New York, Republic, 1924. Also, J. Madge, *Origins of Scientific Sociology*, London, Tavistock, 1963. Madge (pp. 216–17) points out that, although Lindeman coined the term participant observation, it had significantly different meaning then from that in use today (see also pp. 118–19).
18. W. F. Whyte, *Street Corner Society*, Chicago, University of Chicago Press (2nd edn), 1955.
19. E. C. Hughes, *Men and Their Work*, New York, Free Press, 1958.
20. Of the many seminal works of these men that could be quoted we have chosen two: H. S. Becker, *Outsiders*, New York, Collier-Macmillan, 1963; E. Goffman, *Asylums*, Harmondsworth, Penguin, 1963.
21. See, for example, J. Madge, *The Tools of Social Science*, London, Longman, 1953. This is only one of several examples.
22. H. M. Trice, 'The "outsider's" role in field study' in Filstead, op cit.
23. A. Vidich, 'Participant observation and the collection and interpretation of data', *American Journal of Sociology*, **60**, 1955, 354–60.
24. Rock, op. cit., p. 199.
25. Whyte, Street Corner Society.
26. M. A. Sullivan et al., 'Participant observation as employed in the study of a military training programme' in Filstead op. cit., pp. 91–100.
27. Whyte, Street Corner Society, p. 300.
28. Vidich, op. cit.
29. R. L. Gold, 'Roles in sociological field observations', *Social Forces*, **36**, 1958. 217–23. Reprinted in Filstead, op. cit.
30. Ibid.
31. Vidich, op. cit.

32. H. S. Becker, 'Problems of inference and proof in participant observation', *American Sociological Review*, **23**, 1958, 682–90.
33. Ibid., the research examples Becker uses in this article are from his study, *Boys in White*, Chicago, University of Chicago Press, 1961.
34. The most famous of 'control effects' occurred in the Hawthorne experiments. Indeed, such effects are often referred to as 'Hawthorne effects'. We offer some more remarks on this in Chapter 6.
35. W. F. Whyte, 'Observational field-work methods', in M. Jahoda, et al. (eds), *Research Methods in Social Relations*, Vol. 2, New York, Dryden, 1951, pp. 510–11.
36. H. S. Becker and B. Geer, op. cit., p. 141.
37. H. S. Becker, 'Interpretive sociology and constructive typology', in G. Gurvitch and W. E. Moore (eds), *Twentieth Century Sociology*, New York, Philosophical Library, 1945.
36. H. Blumer, 'Society as symbolic interaction' in A. Rose (ed.), *Human Behaviour and Social Processes*, Boston, Houghton Mifflin, 1962, p. 188.
39. M. Schwarz and C. Schwarz, 'Problems in participant observation', *American Journal of Sociology*, **60**, 1955, p. 345.
40. H. Gans, *Urban Villagers*, Glencoe, The Free Press, 1962.
41. J. Lofland, *Analysing Social Settings*, Relmont, Wadsworth, 1971.
42. Whyte, *Street Corner Society*, p. 321.
43. Ibid., p. 301.
44. H. S. Becker, 'Field work evidence' in H. S. Becker, *Sociological Work: Method and Substance*, Chicago, Aldine, 1970.
45. Gans, op. cit.
46. Becker, 'Problems of inference'.
47. Rock, op. cit., especially Ch. 6.
48. Ibid., p. 182.
49. H. Blumer, 'What is wrong with social theory', *American Sociological Review*, **19**, 1954, p. 9.
50. Rock, op. cit., p. 183.
51. Ibid., p. 186.
52. Ibid., p. 187.
53. Vidich, op. cit., p. 357. Also, K. Lang and G. Lang, 'Decisions for Christ: Billy Graham in New York City' in M. Stein et al. (eds), *Identity and Anxiety*, Glencoe, The Free Press, 1960; Rock, op. cit., pp. 200–1.
54. E. C. Hughes, 'Introduction: the place of field work in social science', in B. Turner (ed.), *Fieldwork: An Introduction to the Social Sciences*, Chicago, University of Chicago Press, 1960, p. xi.
55. Rock, op. cit., p. 212. Interestingly, while symbolic interactionism has produced few studies of the 'familiar', to put it this way, ethnomethodology takes as one of its tasks the rendering of the familiar 'strange', in order to investigate the social nature and properties of daily life. See, for example, H. Garfinkel, *Studies in Ethnomethodology*, Englewood Cliffs, Prentice-Hall, 1967.
56. See for further reading, S. Bruyn, *The Human Perspective in Sociology*, New Jersey, Prentice-Hall, 1966; G. Psathas, *Phenomenological Sociology*, New York, Wiley, 1973.
57. Rock, op. cit., p. 201.
58. See, for example, H. S. Becker, 'Field methods and techniques: a note on interviewing tactics', *Human Organisation*, **12**, 1954; Rock, op. cit., p. 201.
59. K. T. Erikson, 'A comment on disguised observation in sociology' in Fils-

tead (ed.) op. cit., p. 253; J. Roth, 'Comment on "Secret observation"', *Social Problems*, **9**, 1962, 283–4.
60. Rock, op. cit., pp. 201–5.
61. See E. Goffman, *The Presentation of Self in Everyday Life*, Harmondsworth, Penguin, 1959.

Chapter 6   The social basis of social research

1. Of course, there are national variations to this general picture and, in addition, variations in the extent to which particular social sciences have succumbed to the state's embrace. Economics, for example, has a far closer association with government than either political science or sociology.
2. See, for example, E. Durkheim, *The Rules of Sociological Method* (trans. G. E. Catlin), Toronto, Collier-Macmillan, 1938, p. 144. Also, S. Lukes, *Emile Durkheim*, Harmondsworth, Penguin, 1973, where sociological knowledge is clearly demarcated as a species of professional expertise.
3. E. Mayo, *Social Problems of Industrial Civilisation*, London, Routledge/and Kegan Paul 1949, p. 21. See also, J. H. Smith, 'Elton Mayo revisited', *British Journal of Industrial Relations*, **12**, 1974.
4. There are exceptions to this general picture, of course; one dramatic example is the use by the US military of social scientists in Vietnam and, rather earlier, to predict and control political systems in Latin America. See, for example, E. Horowitz, *The Rise and Fall of Project Camelot*, Cambridge, Mass., Massachusetts Institute of Technology Press, 1967.
5. For some comments on the development of the human relations approach see S. Ackroyd, 'Sociological theory and the human relations school', *Sociology of Work and Occupations*, **3**, 1976, 379–410.
6. An example of this kind of work is Blalock's on causal modelling, *Causal Inferences in Non Experimental Research*, Chapel Hill, University of North Carolina Press, 1961. Also, papers in H. L. Cosner (ed.), *Sociological Methodology*, New York, Jossey-Bass, 1971.
7. N. K. Denzin, *The Research Act*, Chicago, Aldine, 1970, p. 350. Earlier, C. W. Mills, *The Sociological Imagination*, New York, Oxford University Press, 1959, advocated a similar idea.
8. Denzin, op. cit., p. 313.
9. A. V. Cicourel, *Method and Measurement in Sociology*, New York, The Free Press, 1964; D. Phillips, *Knowledge From What?*, New York, Rand McNally, 1971, and *Abandoning Method*, San Francisco, Jossey-Bass, 1973; P. Filmer et al., *New Directions in Sociological Theory*, London, Collier-Macmillan, 1972.
10. This statement from Oppenheim is especially revealing: 'If it were possible (to get information from the respondent) without asking him any questions, and without the respondent having to "respond" that would be so much the better. ...' See A. N. Oppenheim, *Questionnaire Design and Attitude Measurement*, London, Heinemann, 1966, p. 49.
11. On these maters the selections in R. Turner (ed.), *Ethnomethodology*, Harmondsworth, Penguin, 1974; and A. V. Cicourel, *Cognitive Sociology*, Harmondsworth, Penguin, 1973.
12. See, for example, M. Speier, *How to Observe Face-to Face Communication: A Sociological Introduction* Pacific Palisades, Goodyear, 1973.
13. T. S. Kuhn, *The Structure of Scientific Revolutions*, Chicago, University of Chicago Press (2nd edn), 1970, provides, perhaps unwittingly, a model here.

INDEX